CHOCOLATE COOKBOOK

Cook It Yourself With Chocolate Brownie Cookbook

(Greatest Chocolate Brownie Cookbook of All Time)

Kari Warfield

Published by Alex Howard

© **Kari Warfield**

All Rights Reserved

Chocolate Cookbook: Cook It Yourself With Chocolate Brownie Cookbook (Greatest Chocolate Brownie Cookbook of All Time)

ISBN 978-1-990169-26-7

All rights reserved. No part of this guide may be reproduced in any form without permission in writing from the publisher except in the case of brief quotations embodied in critical articles or reviews.

Legal & Disclaimer

The information contained in this book is not designed to replace or take the place of any form of medicine or professional medical advice. The information in this book has been provided for educational and entertainment purposes only.

The information contained in this book has been compiled from sources deemed reliable, and it is accurate to the best of the Author's knowledge; however, the Author cannot guarantee its accuracy and validity and cannot be held liable for any errors or omissions. Changes are periodically made to this book. You must consult your doctor or get professional medical advice before using any of the suggested remedies, techniques, or information in this book.

Table of contents

PART 1 1

INTRODUCTION 2

Layered Mocha Cheesecake 5
Layered Turtle Cheesecake 8
Lemon Mascarpone Cheesecake 11
Lemon Mousse Cheesecake 14
Light Chocolate Cheesecake 16
Little Orange Dream Cups 18
Luck O' The Irish Cheesecake 20
Luscious Black Forest Cheesecake 22
Makeover Frozen Mocha Cheesecake Loaf 24
Malted Chocolate Cheesecake 26
Mandarin Orange Cheesecake 29
Mint Brownie Cheesecake Cups 31
Mocha Almond Dessert 33
Mocha Cheesecake 35
Mocha Cheesecake Bars 37
Mocha Chip Cheesecake 39
Mocha Chocolate Chip Cheesecake 41
Mocha Truffle Cheesecake 43
Mousse-topped Lime Cheesecake 45
Mudslide Cheesecake 48
Neapolitan Cheesecake 51
New York-style Cheesecake 54
No-bake Cheesecake 56
No-bake Chocolate Cheesecake 59
No-bake Chocolate Chip Cannoli Cheesecake 61
Orange Bliss Cheesecake 63
Orange Chip Cheesecake 65
Orange Chocolate Cheesecake 67
Peanut Butter Cheese Torte 69
Peanut Butter Cheesecake 71
Peanut Butter Cup Cheesecake 73

Pecan-caramel Cheesecake Pie 75
Peppermint Cheesecake On A Stick 77
Peppermint Chip Cheesecake 80
Peppermint Patty Cheesecake... 82

PART 2 84

Pistachio Cheesecake 85
Pressure Cooker Very Vanilla Cheesecake 87
Pumpkin Cheesecake With Sour Cream Topping 89
Quick Chocolate Chip Cheesecake 91
Raspberry & White Chocolate Cheesecake 93
Raspberry Chocolate Cheesecake 96
Raspberry Ribbon Cheesecake 98
Red Velvet Cheesecake 101
Rhubarb Swirl Cheesecake 103
Rich Chocolate Cheesecake 106
Rich Chocolate Mousse Cheesecake 108
S'more Cheesecake... 111
Salted Caramel Cappuccino Cheesecake 113
Special Pleasure Chocolate Cheesecake 116
Spiderweb Cheesecake 118
Spiderweb Pumpkin Cheesecake 120
Strawberries & Cream Pie 122
Swirled Raspberry & Chocolate Cheesecake 124
Taffy Apple Cheesecake Pie 127
Tiny Cherry Cheesecakes.. 129
Toffee Crunch Cheesecake 131
Topped Cheesecake Squares 133
Triple-layer Chocolate Cheesecake 136
Turtle Cheesecake 139
Turtle Pumpkin Cheesecake 141
Tuxedo Cheesecake 143
Two-tone Cheesecake 145
Vanilla Bean Cheesecake With Chocolate Ganache 147
Vanilla Chip Dessert 149
Very Vanilla Slow Cooker Cheesecake 151

White Chocolate Cheesecake	154
White Chocolate Cheesecake With Cherry Topping	156
White Chocolate Cheesecake With Cranberry-orange Compote	158
White Chocolate Lime Mousse Cake	161
White Chocolate Peppermint Cheesecake	163
White Chocolate Pumpkin Cheesecake	165
White Chocolate Pumpkin Cheesecake With Almond Topping	167
White Chocolate Raspberry Cheesecake	169
White Chocolate Strawberry Torte	171
White Chocolate-raspberry Mousse Cheesecake	173
Chocolate Covered Strawberries	176
Creamy Chocolate Covered Strawberries	178
Chocolate Covered Strawberries (2)	179
Chocolate Dipped Strawberries	180
Chocolate Banana Mousse	182
Chocolate Balls	183
Sugar Free Chocolate Nut Clusters	184
Sugar Free Chocolate Butter Creams	185
Bittersweet Chocolate Sauce	187
Chocolate With Chocolate Chip Pancakes	188
Dairy Free Chocolate Pudding	190
Lactose Free Chocolate Cake	191
Dairy Free Chocolate Chip Cookies	192
Dairy Free Hot Chocolate	193

Part 1

Introduction

As a young kid, I helped my mom cook. She would always cook any dish I liked. Observing how she cooked motivated me to try cooking. Ten years later, I'm sharing with you my cooking inspiration as well as the reasons why I love it.

1. Trying something different

Various cuisines of the world use different kinds of ingredients. You can download and share a lot of recipes on the internet. Even so, you can add your own unique twists to recipes and experiment with various versions and styles.

Trying out new recipes and ingredients isn't bad when cooking, as long as you produce something edible…

2. Enjoyment

Whomever you cook for— family, friends, or even yourself—you'll surely have fun doing it. It's satisfying to see how the combination of various spices, meat, and vegetables yield an awesome flavor. From cutting to cooking them, the whole process is nothing but pure joy.

3. Receiving wonderful feedback

Don't you get a sense of pride, joy, and accomplishment when people love the dish you've cooked and let you know their thoughts? You'll definitely savor the moment when you hear someone praise your cooking skills.

Each time someone tells me, "This has a great flavor" or "This is insanely delicious!" I get more motivated to become a better cook…

4. Healthy eating

Rather than consuming processed food, using fresh ingredients for your dishes makes them good for the body. Cook your own meals so that you can add more fresh vegetables and fruits to your diet. Cooking also allows you to discover more about the different nutrients in your meals.

Because you prepare your meals yourself, having digestive problems will be the least of your worries…

5. Therapeutic activity

Based on my experience, cooking calms the mind. Finding food in the fridge, gathering the ingredients, getting them ready, and assembling everything together to create a yummy dish are more relaxing than just spending idle time on the couch watching TV. Cooking never makes me stressed.

My mother would always tell me: Cooking is an edible way to make your loved ones feel loved…

Keeping Up Your Passion for Cooking

Cooking is not for everyone. But people who are passionate about cooking and their families are fortunate indeed. It spreads happiness around. Do you love cooking? Sustain your passion—it's the best feeling ever!

When combined with love, cooking feeds the soul...

From my unending love for cooking, I'm creating this book series and hoping to share my passion with all of you. With my many experiences of failures, I have created this book series and hopefully it helps you. This Ingredient Recipes Series covers these subjects:

- Cheese Recipes
- Butter Recipes
- Red Wine Recipes
- Cajun Spice Recipes
- Mayonnaise Recipes

Layered Mocha Cheesecake

""Ended up mixing a few of my favorite recipes to make this yummy version when I was looking for the perfect mocha cheesecake. Surely will satisfy your palate!""
Serving: 16 servings. | Prep: 30m | Ready in: 01h30m

Ingredients

- 1-1/2 cups Oreo cookie crumbs
- 1/4 cup butter, melted
- FILLING:
- 2 tbsps. plus 1-1/2 tsps. instant coffee granules
- 1 tbsp. hot water
- 1/4 tsp. ground cinnamon
- 4 packages (8 oz. each) cream cheese, softened
- 1-1/2 cups sugar
- 1/4 cup all-purpose flour
- 2 tsps. vanilla extract
- 4 large eggs, lightly beaten
- 2 cups (12 oz.) semisweet chocolate chips, melted and cooled
- GLAZE:
- 1/2 cup semisweet chocolate chips
- 3 tbsps. butter
- Chocolate-covered coffee beans, optional

Direction

- Put a 9-inch springform pan that is greased on a double thickness of heavy-duty foil (about 18 inches square).Tightly wrap foil around pan. In a small bowl, mix cookie crumbs and butter; press onto the bottom of prepared pan.
- Combine cinnamon, hot water, and coffee granules in another bowl; reserve. Beat vanilla, flour, sugar and cream cheese in a large bowl until turns smooth. Put in eggs; whisk on low speed just until mixed. Split batter in half. Mix melted chocolate into one portion; place over crust. Mix coffee mixture into the remaining batter; scoop over chocolate layer. Put springform pan in a large baking pan; put in 1-inch of hot water to larger pan. Place in the oven and bake for 60-65 minutes at 325°F or until middle is just set and top looks dull. Take the springform pan from water bath; take off the foil. Place cheesecake on wire rack and cool for 10 minutes; use a knife to loosen sides from pan. Let it cool for 1 more hour. Place in the refrigerator overnight. Take the rim from pan. To make glaze, melt butter and chocolate chips in a microwave; mix until turns smooth; place over cheesecake and spread. If desired, put coffee beans on top.

Nutrition Information
- Calories: 535 calories
- Total Carbohydrate: 48 g
- Cholesterol: 128 mg
- Total Fat: 37 g
- Fiber: 2 g

- Protein: 8 g
- Sodium: 295 mg

Layered Turtle Cheesecake

"This is a special turtle cheesecake that is definitely a crowd favorite."

Serving: 12 servings. | Prep: 40m | Ready in: 01h55m

Ingredients

- 1 cup all-purpose flour
- 1/3 cup packed brown sugar
- 1/4 cup finely chopped pecans
- 6 tbsps. cold butter, cubed
- FILLING:
- 4 packages (8 oz. each) cream cheese, softened
- 1 cup sugar
- 1/3 cup packed brown sugar
- 1/4 cup plus 1 tsp. all-purpose flour, divided
- 2 tbsps. heavy whipping cream
- 1-1/2 tsps. vanilla extract
- 4 eggs, lightly beaten
- 1/2 cup milk chocolate chips, melted and cooled
- 1/4 cup caramel ice cream topping
- 1/3 cup chopped pecans
- GANACHE:
- 1/2 cup milk chocolate chips
- 1/4 cup heavy whipping cream
- 2 tbsps. chopped pecans
- Additional caramel ice cream topping, optional

Direction

- Firmly cover the greased 9-inch springform pan with an 18-inch square of double thickness heavy-duty foil.
- Mix pecans, brown sugar and flour in a small bowl; add butter and cut in until texture is crumbly. Compress mixture onto the base of the pan. On a baking sheet, place the pan. Put inside the oven and bake for 12-15 minutes at 325°F or until it has set. Transfer to a wire rack and let it to cool down.
- Whip sugars and cream cheese in a big bowl until smooth in texture. Mix in vanilla, cream, and 1/4 cup of flour. Put in eggs; on low speed whip the eggs until mixed evenly. Take out 1 cup of batter and put in a small bowl. Add in chocolate that is melted. Distribute evenly on top of the crust.
- Combine the rest of the flour with caramel topping in a separate bowl. Mix in the pecans. Add the mixture on top of the chocolate batter by tablespoonfuls. Add the remaining batter on top. In a large baking pan, put the springform pan; put an inch of hot water in the baking pan.
- Put inside the oven and bake for 1-1/4 to 1-1/2 hours at 325°F or until the middle has just set and top looks dull. Take out from water bath the springform pan; take off the foil. Transfer to a wire rack and cool the cheesecake for 10 minutes. Loosen the cake by running a knife cautiously around the pan's edges; let it cool for another 1 hour. Put in refrigerator for a night.
- In making ganache, put chips into a small bowl. Bring cream just to a boil in a small saucepan. Dump on top

of the chips; mix until smooth in consistency. Let it cool for a bit, mixing occasionally.

• Remove springform pan's sides. Pour ganache over cheesecake evenly; drizzle with pecans. Put in refrigerator until it sets. If you want, add a caramel topping by drizzling before serving.

Nutrition Information

- Calories: 664 calories
- Total Carbohydrate: 55 g
- Cholesterol: 182 mg
- Total Fat: 46 g
- Fiber: 2 g
- Protein: 11 g
- Sodium: 330 mg

Lemon Mascarpone Cheesecake

"Your family and friends will surely request for this sweet treat after tasting it. Best treat for Easter because of its mild lemon flavor and light in color."
Serving: 14 servings. | Prep: 30m | Ready in: 01h15m

Ingredients

- 1-1/2 cups biscotti crumbs (about 8 biscotti)
- 1/3 cup butter, melted
- FILLING:
- 2 packages (8 oz. each) cream cheese, softened
- 2 cartons (8 oz. each) Mascarpone cheese
- 3/4 cup sugar
- 1/4 cup lemon juice
- 3 tbsps. all-purpose flour
- 1 tbsp. grated lemon peel
- 2 tsps. vanilla extract
- 4 eggs, lightly beaten
- TOPPING:
- 3/4 cup coarsely chopped dried apricots
- 1/2 cup boiling water
- 3/4 cup cold water
- 1/4 cup sugar
- 1/4 cup orange marmalade
- 2 oz. white baking chocolate

Direction

- Mix butter and biscotti crumbs in a small bowl. Grease a 9-inch springform pan, then press the mixture up sides 1 inch and on the bottom of pan.
- Set it on a baking pan and let it bake at 350°F. Bake it for 8 to 10 minutes until it turns to light brown.
- Beat sugar and cheeses in a large bowl until smooth. Mix in the flour, lemon juice, vanilla and lemon peel. Add the eggs and on low speed beat until just combined. Transfer the mixture into the crust.
- Bake it again at 350°F for about 45 to 55 minutes until the center is nearly set. Let it cool for at least 10 minutes on a wire rack. Loosen from pan by running a knife around the edges. Let it rest to cool for a half an hour.
- In the meantime, for 10 minutes immerse apricots in boiling water. Drain the water and discard it. Add cold water, sugar and the apricots in a small saucepan and boil. Decrease heat, do not cover, and simmer until the water is completely absorbed, 12-14 minutes. Take off the heat and add marmalade. Let it cool down to room temperature.
- Drizzle the toppings on top of cheesecake and let it cool for 30 minutes more. Place it in refrigerator overnight.
- Melt white chocolate in a microwave. Stir it until smooth before sprinkling it on top of cheesecake. Let it rest for 15 minutes. Be sure to refrigerate leftovers.

Nutrition Information

- Calories: 347 calories

- Total Carbohydrate: 35 g
- Cholesterol: 114 mg
- Total Fat: 21 g
- Fiber: 1 g
- Protein: 6 g
- Sodium: 173 mg

Lemon Mousse Cheesecake

"Candlelight, music and this dessert - perfect setting for your special intimate dinner."
Serving: 4 servings. | Prep: 20m | Ready in: 60m

Ingredients

- 1/2 cup crushed chocolate wafers (about 8 wafers)
- 2 tbsps. butter, melted
- 1 package (8 oz.) cream cheese, softened
- 1/2 cup sugar
- 1/2 cup sour cream
- 1 tbsp. all-purpose flour
- 1 egg, lightly beaten
- 3 tbsps. lemon juice
- 1 tbsp. grated lemon peel
- 1/2 tsp. vanilla extract

Direction

- Preheat oven to 325 degrees and coat a 6-inch springform pan with cooking spray. Combine chocolate wafers and butter in a small bowl. Press mixture onto the bottom of the springform pan then set pan on top of a baking sheet and bake for 10 minutes. Set aside and let it cool on a wire rack.
- Meanwhile, combine sugar and cream cheese in a large bowl. Beat together until you achieve a smooth

consistency. Add flour and sour cream, blend well. Add egg and beat on low speed just until incorporated. Lastly, stir in vanilla, lemon juice and peel just until mixed. Pour mixture over the prepared crust.

• Take the pan back to the baking sheet and bake for 40 to 45 minutes or until the center nearly set. Set aside and let it cool on a wire rack for 10 minutes. Then carefully loosen the edge of the pan by running a knife around the edge. Let the cake cool for another 1 hour then keep refrigerated overnight; refrigerate leftovers.

Nutrition Information

- Calories: 487 calories
- Total Carbohydrate: 39 g
- Cholesterol: 151 mg
- Total Fat: 33 g
- Fiber: 1 g
- Protein: 8 g
- Sodium: 327 mg

Light Chocolate Cheesecake

""This low-fat chocolate cheesecake is unbelievably light your craving for sweets will be fulfilled with just a small portion.""

Serving: 10 servings. | Prep: 15m | Ready in: 40m

Ingredients

- 2 whole chocolate graham crackers, crushed
- 1/4 cup fat-free half-and-half
- 12 oz. reduced-fat cream cheese
- 1 cup (8 oz.) fat-free cottage cheese
- 1 cup sugar
- 6 tbsps. baking cocoa
- 1/4 cup all-purpose flour
- 1 tsp. vanilla extract
- 1/4 cup egg substitute
- 1/4 cup miniature semisweet chocolate chips
- 1/2 oz. white baking chocolate, shaved
- 1/2 oz. semisweet chocolate, shaved

Direction

- Using a cooking spray, grease the springform pan, 9-inch in size. Dust the pan with bread crumbs; reserve. In a food processor, put in half-and-half, cottage cheese, cream cheese, vanilla, flour, cocoa, and sugar. Process with the cover on until the consistency is smooth. In a large bowl, put inside the processed mixture and beat in egg substitute. Add in chocolate

chips and lightly mix by folding. Put mixture into the pan and lay on a baking sheet.
• Put inside the oven and bake for 25-30 minutes at 325°F or until it is nearly set. Transfer to a wire rack and let cool for 10 minutes. Loosen the cake by running a knife cautiously around the pan and cool for another 1 hour or longer. Put inside the refrigerator for the night. Add shaved chocolate all over the top of the cake. Store leftovers the refrigerator.

Nutrition Information
- Calories: 243 calories
- Total Carbohydrate: 35 g
- Cholesterol: 20 mg
- Total Fat: 9 g
- Fiber: 2 g
- Protein: 9 g
- Sodium: 238 mg

Little Orange Dream Cups

"These velvety flavored orange cups are made with lower fat dairy products and guaranteed fat-free. Instead of using chocolate water, use gingersnaps as substitute for a crispier variation." Serving: 1 dozen. | Prep: 30m | Ready in: 30m

Ingredients

- 1 envelope unflavored gelatin
- 3/4 cup fat-free milk
- 1 package (8 oz.) fat-free cream cheese
- 1 cup reduced-fat sour cream
- Sugar substitute equivalent to 1/4 cup sugar
- 3/4 tsp. grated orange zest
- 1/2 tsp. vanilla extract
- 1 carton (8 oz.) frozen reduced-fat whipped topping, thawed, divided
- 12 chocolate wafers

Direction

- Sprinkle gelatin over milk in a small saucepan and let it stand for 1 minute. Heat on low heat and stir until the gelatin is melted completely. Take away from the heat and let it cool a little.
- Beat the sour cream, cream cheese, orange zest, vanilla and sugar substitute in a small bowl until it becomes smooth. Slowly blend in the gelatin mixture. Fold in 2 cups whipped topping.

- Line muffin cups with foil, then put chocolate wafers. Place 1/2 cup cream cheese mixture on top of each muffin. Place in the refrigerator for 2 hours or until set. Carefully peel the foil then serve; embellish with the leftover whipped topping.

Nutrition Information
- Calories: 123 calories
- Total Carbohydrate: 12 g
- Cholesterol: 9 mg
- Total Fat: 5 g
- Fiber: 0 g
- Protein: 5 g
- Sodium: 160 mg

Luck O' The Irish Cheesecake

""This recipe is a spotlight of the St.Patrick's Day party in our family. I serves this classic cheesecake every year all of us look forward to. I was happy when someone shared this recipe to me. The mix of peppermint and chocolate instantly turns a favorite of everyone who tries it.""
Serving: 8-10 servings. | Prep: 40m | Ready in: 01h40m

Ingredients

- 20 Oreo cookies, crushed
- 3 tbsps. butter, melted
- 3 packages (8 oz. each) cream cheese, softened
- 1 can (14 oz.) sweetened condensed milk
- 1 tsp. peppermint extract
- 6 drops green food coloring
- 3 eggs, lightly beaten
- 1 cup miniature chocolate chips, divided

Direction

- Mix butter and cookie crumbs; then push down onto the bottom of a greased 9-inch springform pan. Mix food coloring, extract, milk and cream cheese in a bowl until smooth. Put in eggs; whisk on low speed just until mixed. Mix in 1/2 cup chocolate chips.
- Put onto crust. Put the pan on a baking sheet. Place in the oven and bake for 1 hour at 300°F or until middle is just set. Cool for 10 minutes on a wire rack; use a

knife to run around edge of pan to loosen. Cool for 1 more hour. Keep for overnight in the refrigerator. Mark a small shamrock pattern onto a piece of paper; cut out and reserve. Melt remaining chocolate chips in a microwave. Then fill plastic bag with melted chocolate; cut a small hole in a corner of the bag. Put shamrock pattern on a baking sheet; put a large piece of waxed paper over pattern. Onto shamrock waxed paper, pipe a chocolate, following the pattern. And move waxed paper and repeat to create a several more shamrocks.
• Put in the freezer for about 4 minutes until firm. Gently take out shamrocks and pile on cheesecake.

Nutrition Information
- Calories: 451 calories
- Total Carbohydrate: 49 g
- Cholesterol: 111 mg
- Total Fat: 26 g
- Fiber: 2 g
- Protein: 9 g
- Sodium: 320 mg

Luscious Black Forest Cheesecake

""This recipe was handed to me by a friend and it's instantly become popular at our home. I love preparing it when we entertain. My hubby and I are dairy farmers and have 3 kids. I love testing new recipes as well as crafts and yardworks.""
Serving: 12-16 servings. | Prep: 40m | Ready in: 40m

Ingredients

- 1-1/4 cups chocolate wafer crumbs
- 1/4 cup butter, melted
- 2 envelopes unflavored gelatin
- 1 cup cold water
- 1 can (21 oz.) cherry pie filling
- 1/2 tsp. almond extract
- 2 packages (8 oz. each) cream cheese, softened
- 1/3 cup sugar
- 2 oz. semisweet chocolate, melted and cooled
- 1 tsp. brandy extract or vanilla extract
- 1 cup heavy whipping cream, whipped
- Maraschino cherries and additional whipped cream and melted chocolate for garnish, optional

Direction

- Combine butter and crumbs; then press into the bottom and up the sides of a 9-inch springform pan. Let chill for 15 minutes.

• Sprinkle gelatin over cold water in a small saucepan; allow to stand for 1 minute. Then heat over low heat, whisking until gelatin is fully melted. Combine almond extract and 1/3 cup gelatin mixture with pie filling; place into crust and chill until set.
• Whip sugar and cream cheese in a large bowl until smooth. Mix in the remaining gelatin mixture, brandy extract and melted chocolate. Add whipped cream then fold; and spread over cherry layer. Let chill for at least 3 hours.
• Take from pan. Decorate with the cherries, chocolate and whipped cream if wished.

Nutrition Information

- Calories: 211 calories
- Total Carbohydrate: 23 g
- Cholesterol: 34 mg
- Total Fat: 12 g
- Fiber: 1 g
- Protein: 3 g
- Sodium: 133 mg

Makeover Frozen Mocha Cheesecake Loaf

"This innovative frosty mocha cheesecake loaf has calories fewer than the original. The cholesterol level is down to 72% and fat down to 60%."
Serving: 12 servings. | Prep: 30m | Ready in: 30m

Ingredients

- 1-1/2 cups reduced-fat Oreo cookie crumbs
- 4-1/2 tsps. butter, melted
- 1 package (8 oz.) reduced-fat cream cheese
- 1 can (14 oz.) fat-free sweetened condensed milk
- 1 tbsp. vanilla extract
- 4 cups reduced-fat whipped topping
- 7 tsps. instant coffee granules
- 1 tbsp. hot water
- 1/2 cup chocolate syrup

Direction

- Prepare a 9x5 inch loaf pan then line with heavy-duty foil. Mix butter and cookie crumbs in a small bowl. On the bottom and 1/2 inches up the sides of the prepared pan, press down the mixture firmly.
- Beat cream cheese until it becomes fluffy and light in a big bowl. Mix in vanilla and milk; stir well. Fold in whipped topping. In another bowl, scoop half of the mixture then put aside. In a hot water, melt coffee granules then fold into the leftover cream cheese mixture. Fold in chocolate syrup.

- Scoop half of the chocolate mixture over the crust. Then use half of the reserved cream cheese mixture as topping. Repeat the layering process (pan should be full). Put in the freezer, remove cover for 6 hours or until set. Put cover, freeze, and then serve. Remove from pan using a foil then slice.

Nutrition Information
- Calories: 299 calories
- Total Carbohydrate: 45 g
- Cholesterol: 19 mg
- Total Fat: 10 g
- Fiber: 1 g
- Protein: 6 g
- Sodium: 219 mg

Malted Chocolate Cheesecake

"This affordable but expensive-looking dessert will make you feel special because of its elegant appearance and luscious malt flavor."
Serving: 2 servings. | Prep: 30m | Ready in: 01h10m

Ingredients

- 4 portions refrigerated ready-to-bake sugar cookie dough
- 4 oz. cream cheese, softened
- 1/2 cup dark chocolate chips, melted
- 2 tbsps. sugar
- 1 large egg white
- 1/2 tsp. vanilla extract
- TOPPING:
- 4-1/2 tsps. cream cheese, softened
- 2 tsps. sugar
- 1 tsp. malted milk powder
- 1 tsp. baking cocoa
- 2/3 cup whipped topping
- 1 tbsp. chocolate syrup

Direction

- Use foil to line a 5 3/4 x3x2 inch loaf pan. Place the cookie dough on the bottom. Bake it at 325°F for 15 to

20 minutes until it is golden brown in color. Let it cool on a wire rack.
- Whisk the melted chocolate, sugar and cream cheese in a small bowl until smooth. Add the egg white and whisk on low speed until just mixed. Stir the vanilla in; then dump it over the crust.
- Set the loaf pan in a baking pan and add 1 inch of water to the baking pan. Let it bake at 325°F for 40 to 45 minutes until the top looks dull and the center has just set.
- Remove the pan from the water bath and set it on a wire rack to cool, 10 minutes. Loosen from the pan by running a knife around the edges. Let it cool for another hour.
- Store it in the refrigerator overnight. Mix in a small bowl until smooth, the sugar, baking cocoa, cream cheese and milk powder to create topping. Add by folding the whipped topping before spreading it over the cheesecake. Seal it before storing in the refrigerator for 60 minutes.
- Remove the cheesecake from the pan using the inserted foil. Divide it in half and sprinkle each with chocolate syrup. Be sure to refrigerate any leftovers.

Nutrition Information
- Calories: 934 calories
- Total Carbohydrate: 92 g
- Cholesterol: 74 mg
- Total Fat: 58 g
- Fiber: 0 g

- Protein: 14 g
- Sodium: 350 mg

Mandarin Orange Cheesecake

"Try this mini homemade cheesecake with a blend of cream cheese, chocolate and orange taste!" Serving: 4 servings. | Prep: 20m | Ready in: 25m

Ingredients

- 1/2 cup crushed chocolate wafers (about 8 wafers)
- 2 tbsps. butter, melted
- 4-1/2 tsps. sugar
- 4 oz. cream cheese, softened
- 1 tbsp. orange marmalade
- 1 cup whipped topping
- 1 can (11 oz.) mandarin oranges, drained

Direction

- Combine butter, sugar and wafer crumbs in a bowl. In an ungreased 6-inch springform pan, press mixture on bottom and 1/2 inch up the sides; place on baking tray. Bake for 5 minutes at 375 degrees. Let cool on a wire rack.
- Blend cream cheese and marmalade in a small bowl. Fold in the whipped topping. Place 2/3 of oranges on the crust. Spread cream cheese mixture on top. Garnish with remaining oranges. Chill for 2 hours.

Nutrition Information

- Calories: 213 calories

- Total Carbohydrate: 27 g
- Cholesterol: 30 mg
- Total Fat: 10 g
- Fiber: 0 g
- Protein: 5 g
- Sodium: 196 mg

Mint Brownie Cheesecake Cups

"Serve this fuss-free brownie cheesecake, with a hint of some mint chocolate, at any of your gatherings. Your guests will sure love and talk about this beautiful recipe."

Serving: 2-1/2 dozen. | Prep: 20m | Ready in: 45m

Ingredients

- 1/2 cup crushed chocolate cream-filled chocolate sandwich cookies (about 7 cookies)
- 1 package (4.67 oz.) Andes mint candies or 1 cup Andes creme de menthe baking chips
- 1 package (8 oz.) cream cheese, softened
- 1/4 cup sugar
- 1 egg
- 1/2 tsp. vanilla extract
- Additional Andes mint candies or Andes creme de menthe baking chips, melted

Direction

- Line or grease miniature muffin cups. Put 1 tsp. of cookie crumbs onto each muffin cup bottom, and then set it aside.
- For 30 seconds to 1 minute, heat the candies in a microwave-safe bowl, mixing it every 15 seconds, until it's completely melted. Let it cool to room temperature.

- Mix, until smooth, sugar and cream cheese in a small bowl. Stir in vanilla and egg. Mix the melted candies in.
- In each muffin cup, put 1 tbsp. of the mixture. Let it bake at 350°F 25 to 30 minutes until each top begins to crack and looks dry. Let muffins rest for about 60 seconds before removing from pan and putting them on wire racks to completely cooling. Sprinkle some more melted candies before storing in the fridge.

Nutrition Information

- Calories: 67 calories
- Total Carbohydrate: 6 g
- Cholesterol: 14 mg
- Total Fat: 5 g
- Fiber: 0 g
- Protein: 1 g
- Sodium: 35 mg

Mocha Almond Dessert

""Try this recipe for a simple, make-ahead dessert that's wonderful and yummy. The perfect mix of chocolate and mocha is in each cool, invigorating slice.""

Serving: 10-12 servings. | Prep: 20m | Ready in: 20m

Ingredients

- 2 cups cream-filled chocolate sandwich cookie crumbs
- 1/2 cup sugar
- 1/2 cup butter, melted
- 1 cup heavy whipping cream
- 1 package (8 oz.) cream cheese, softened
- 1 can (14 oz.) sweetened condensed milk
- 2/3 cup chocolate syrup
- 1/2 tsp. vanilla extract
- 2 tbsps. instant coffee granules
- 1 tbsp. hot water
- 1/3 cup chopped almonds, toasted
- Chocolate-covered coffee beans, optional

Direction

- Mix butter, sugar and cookie crumbs in a small bowl. Then press onto the bottom and 1 in up the sides of a 9-inch springform pan that is greased; reserve. Beat cream in a large bowl until form a stiff peaks. Beat the vanilla, chocolate syrup, milk and cream cheese in a separate large bowl until turns smooth. Melt coffee granules in hot water; whisk into cream cheese mixture. Fold in almonds and whipped cream. Place over crust. Freeze for 8 hours or overnight, covered. Take from the freezer 10-15 minutes prior serving. Cautiously run a knife around edge of pan to loose. Decorate with coffee beans if you want.

Nutrition Information
- Calories: 366 calories
- Total Carbohydrate: 44 g
- Cholesterol: 42 mg
- Total Fat: 19 g
- Fiber: 2 g
- Protein: 6 g
- Sodium: 209 mg

Mocha Cheesecake

"This very reliable dessert has never let me down whenever a company comes around. Plus, it's very easy to make."

Serving: 8-10 servings. | Prep: 35m | Ready in: 55m

Ingredients

- 1-1/4 cups confectioners' sugar
- 1 cup all-purpose flour
- 1/2 cup baking cocoa
- 1/4 tsp. baking soda
- Dash salt
- 1/2 cup butter, melted
- FILLING:
- 1 package (8 oz.) cream cheese, softened
- 1 can (14 oz.) sweetened condensed milk
- 2 eggs, lightly beaten
- 1 tbsp. hot water
- 2 to 3 tsps. instant coffee granules
- Chocolate-covered coffee beans and whipped topping, optional

Direction

- Mix the first five ingredients and butter in a bowl. In 9-inch greased springform pan, Press onto the bottom and 1 inch up the sides of the pan. Put pan on a baking sheet. Place inside the oven and bake for about 12-15

minutes or until edges become brown at 350 degrees. Transfer on a wire rack to cool.
- Beat until smooth the milk and cream cheese in a big bowl. Then add the eggs, beating on low speed just until combined. Mix coffee granules and water in a small bowl and wait for 1 minute to stand. Stir into the creamed mixture and beat until just combined. Transfer into crust. Put back the pan into the baking sheet.
- Place inside the oven and bake until center is nearly set for about 20-25 minutes at 350 degrees. Transfer on a wire rack and let it cool for 10 minutes. Use a knife and gently run around the pan's edges to loosen; cool for 1 more hour. Chill overnight.
- Take out sides of the pan. Let it sit for 30 minutes at room temperature then cut. Put whipped topping and chocolate-covered coffee beans on top if desired. Store leftovers in the refrigerator.

Nutrition Information
- Calories: 418 calories
- Total Carbohydrate: 49 g
- Cholesterol: 105 mg
- Total Fat: 22 g
- Fiber: 1 g
- Protein: 8 g
- Sodium: 269 mg

Mocha Cheesecake Bars

"This simple recipe makes a rich and yummy filling. A cheesecake with only few ingredients."
Serving: 24 servings. | Prep: 30m | Ready in: 30m

Ingredients

- 25 reduced-fat Oreo cookies,
- 3 tbsps. fat-free hot fudge ice cream topping
- 3 tbsps. butter, melted
- FILLING:
- 1 envelope unflavored gelatin
- 1/2 cup cold strong brewed coffee
- 2 packages (8 oz. each) reduced-fat cream cheese
- 3/4 cup sugar
- 1 cup (8 oz.) reduced-fat sour cream
- 3 oz. bittersweet chocolate, melted and cooled
- 24 chocolate-covered coffee beans, optional

Direction

- Using a food processor, pulse cookies into fine crumbs. Put in butter and fudge topping and pulse again until mixed. In a 13x9 dish, spritz with cooking spray. Press mixture into bottom and chill for 10 minutes.
- For filling, drizzle gelatin over coffee in a saucepan and let sit for 1 minute. Dissolve gelatin on low heat while constantly stirring. Take off heat and set aside.

- Mix sugar and cream cheese until smooth in a bowl. Add in chocolate, sour cream, and coffee mixture beat until combined. Put mixture in crust. Chill, covered, for 4 or more hours or until firm.
- Cut in squares. Decorate with coffee beans, if you want. Chill remaining squares.

Nutrition Information

- Calories: 166 calories
- Total Carbohydrate: 20 g
- Cholesterol: 20 mg
- Total Fat: 9 g
- Fiber: 1 g
- Protein: 4 g
- Sodium: 167 mg

Mocha Chip Cheesecake

""Chocolate and coffee are my two favorite flavors; mix in this treat. The sprinkling of mini cups and chocolate crumb crust contrast nicely with the creamy coffee filling.""

Serving: 12-14 servings. | Prep: 20m | Ready in: 01h10m

Ingredients

- CRUST:
- 2 cups chocolate wafer crumbs (about 32 wafers)
- 1/2 cup sugar
- 1/2 cup butter, melted
- FILLING:
- 3 packages (8 oz. each) cream cheese, softened
- 1 cup sugar
- 3 tbsps. all-purpose flour
- 4 eggs, lightly beaten
- 1/3 cup heavy whipping cream
- 1 tbsp. instant coffee granules
- 1 tsp. vanilla extract
- 1 cup (6 oz.) miniature semisweet chocolate chips, divided

Direction

- Mix sugar and crumbs in a large bowl; mix in butter. Push onto the bottom and 2-inch up the sides of 9-inch springform pan that is greased; reserve. Beat sugar and cream cheese in a large bowl until become smooth. Put in flour and mix well. Mix in eggs, mixing on low speed just until mixed. Mix coffee granules and cream in a small bowl; allow to stand for 1 minutes. Put into cream cheese mixture with vanilla; whisk just until mixed. Mix in 3/4 cup chocolate chips. Put into crust. Dust with remaining chocolate chips. Place in the oven and bake for 50-55 minutes at 325°F or until middle is almost set. Place on a wire rack and cool for 1 hour. Place in the refrigerator for overnight. Allow to stand at a room temperature for 30 minutes prior slicing.

Nutrition Information

- Calories: 314 calories
- Total Carbohydrate: 35 g
- Cholesterol: 104 mg
- Total Fat: 18 g
- Fiber: 1 g
- Protein: 4 g
- Sodium: 227 mg

Mocha Chocolate Chip Cheesecake

"This is one of my mother's extraordinary pastries, which she regularly served on our dining table. Its taste brings back my childhood memories."
Serving: 16 servings. | Prep: 60m | Ready in: 03h00m

Ingredients

- 1-1/2 cups chocolate wafer crumbs
- 1/3 cup sugar
- 6 tbsps. butter, melted
- FILLING:
- 1/2 cup heavy whipping cream
- 1 tbsp. instant coffee granules
- 3 packages (8 oz. each) cream cheese, softened
- 1 cup sugar
- 1 tsp. vanilla extract
- 3 large eggs, lightly beaten
- 1 cup (6 oz.) miniature semisweet chocolate chips, divided

Direction

- Grease a 9-inches springform pan and place it over a double thickness of heavy-duty foil, about 18-inches square. Wrap the foil around the pan tightly.
- Mix butter, wafer crumbs, and sugar in a big bowl and spread it on the prepared pan.

• Combine the coffee granules and cream in a small saucepan. Cook the granules, stirring constantly until it dissolves completely. Allow it to cool.
• Whisk cream cheese and sugar in a big bowl until smooth. Add vanilla and the coffee mixture. Beat in eggs and whisk at low speed just until incorporated. Blend in a 3/4 cup of chocolate chips. Pour the mixture over the crust and top it with the remaining chocolate chips. Pour hot water into a big baking pan, about 1-inch of the pan. Place the springform pan into the water bath.
• Set the oven to 325°F and let it bake for 60-70 minutes until the cake's top appears dull and its center is fixed. Remove the pan from the water bath and transfer it on a wire rack to cool for 10 minutes. Run a knife slowly around the edges of the pan to loosen the cake. Let it cool for 1 more hour. Store it inside the fridge overnight. Remove the rim from the pan before serving.

Nutrition Information
• Calories: 388 calories
• Total Carbohydrate: 33 g
• Cholesterol: 108 mg
• Total Fat: 28 g
• Fiber: 1 g
• Protein: 6 g
• Sodium: 234 mg

Mocha Truffle Cheesecake

"This dessert is ideal for the coffee and cheesecake lover. Perfect for reunions because it can be made ahead of time."
Serving: 16 servings. | Prep: 20m | Ready in: 01h10m

Ingredients

- 1 package devil's food cake mix (regular size)
- 6 tbsps. butter, melted
- 1 large egg
- 1 to 3 tbsps. instant coffee granules
- FILLING/TOPPING:
- 2 packages (8 oz. each) cream cheese, softened
- 1 can (14 oz.) sweetened condensed milk
- 2 cups (12 oz.) semisweet chocolate chips, melted and cooled
- 3 to 6 tbsps. instant coffee granules
- 1/4 cup hot water
- 3 large eggs, lightly beaten
- 1 cup heavy whipping cream
- 1/4 cup confectioners' sugar
- 1/2 tsp. almond extract
- 1 tbsp. baking cocoa, optional

Direction

- Mix coffee granules, egg, butter and cake mix in a big bowl until well combined. In a greased 10-inch springform pan, add the mixture and compress onto the base of the pan and 2 inches up all sides.
- Whip cream cheese in a separate large bowl until smooth in texture. Whip melted chips and milk. Stir coffee granules in water to dissolve. Put coffee into cream cheese mixture. Mix in eggs; whip on low speed until just mixed. Put on the crust. Put pan on a baking sheet.
- Put inside the oven and bake for 50-55 minutes at 325°F or until middle has almost set. Transfer to a wire rack to cool for 10 minutes. Loosen the cake by running a knife cautiously around the pan's edges; let it cool for another hour. Refrigerate to chill for a night.
- Before serving, whip cream in a large bowl, until soft peaks appear. Mix in extract and sugar until firm peaks are formed. Put on top of the cheesecake and distribute evenly. If you want, drizzle with cocoa. Keep leftovers in refrigerator.

Nutrition Information

- Calories: 484 calories
- Total Carbohydrate: 55 g
- Cholesterol: 109 mg
- Total Fat: 28 g
- Fiber: 2 g
- Protein: 7 g
- Sodium: 389 mg

Mousse-topped Lime Cheesecake

""I made this delicious cheesecake by mixing a few different dessert ideas. Chocolate pairs well with the tropical tastes of coconut and lime.""
Serving: 12 servings. | Prep: 60m | Ready in: 01h30m

Ingredients

- 1-1/2 cups crushed chocolate graham crackers
- 1/2 cup sweetened shredded coconut, toasted
- 2 tbsps. sugar
- 1/3 cup butter, melted
- FILLING:
- 2 packages (8 oz. each) cream cheese, softened
- 3/4 cup sugar
- 1/4 cup lime juice
- 3 tbsps. all-purpose flour
- 1 tbsp. grated lime zest
- 1 tsp. vanilla extract
- 2 drops green food coloring, optional
- 2 large eggs, separated
- TOPPING:
- 1 cup semisweet chocolate chips
- 5 tbsps. butter, cubed
- 4 large egg yolks
- 1/4 cup confectioners' sugar
- 2 tbsps. hot brewed coffee
- 1 tsp. vanilla extract
- 1/2 cup heavy whipping cream

Direction

• Mix in a bowl the sugar, coconut and cracker crumbs; mix in butter. Then press onto the bottom and 1-inch up the sides of a 9-inch springform pan that is greased. Put on a baking sheet. Place in the oven and bake for 7-9 minutes at 350°F. Put the pan on a wire rack. Lower heat to 325°F.

• To make filling, beat sugar and cream cheese in a large bowl until smooth. Mix in the vanilla, zest, flour and lime juice and food coloring if wished.

• Mix in egg yolks; whisk on low speed until mixed. Beat egg whites in a small bowl until form a stiff peaks; then fold into filling. Place into crust. Put the pan back to baking sheet. Then bake in the oven for 30-35 minutes or until middle is just set. Place and cool on a wire rack for 10 minutes. Cautiously run a knife around edge of pan to loosen. Cool for 1 more hour. Keep for overnight in the refrigerator.

• To make topping, melt butter and chocolate chips in a microwave; mix until smooth. Reserve. Combine in a heavy saucepan the coffee, confectioner's sugar and egg yolks. Stir and cook over low heat until mixture becomes thick and reaches at least 160°F and covers the back of metal spoon. Separate from heat. Mix in vanilla and chocolate mixture. Let fully cool.

• Whisk whipping cream until forms a soft peaks; fold into topping. Then place over cheesecake and spread. Place in the refrigerator for at least 2 hours or until set.

Nutrition Information

- Calories: 426 calories
- Total Carbohydrate: 39 g
- Cholesterol: 167 mg
- Total Fat: 29 g
- Fiber: 1 g
- Protein: 5 g
- Sodium: 248 mg

Mudslide Cheesecake

"Add different liqueur flavorings to level up cheesecake recipes. This favorite recipe is a "mudslide" version that uses coffee and Irish cream."
Serving: 16 servings. | Prep: 30m | Ready in: 01h30m

Ingredients

- 1 cup chocolate wafer crumbs
- 3 tbsps. sugar
- 2 tbsps. butter, melted
- FILLING:
- 1 cup (6 oz.) semisweet chocolate chips
- 4 packages (8 oz. each) cream cheese, softened
- 1-1/2 cups sugar
- 4 tbsps. all-purpose flour
- 4 large eggs, room temperature
- 2 tsps. vanilla extract
- 2 tbsps. coffee liqueur
- 3/4 cup Irish cream liqueur
- GANACHE:
- 1/2 cup (3 oz.) semisweet chocolate chips
- 1/4 cup heavy whipping cream

Direction

• Set oven to 325 degrees and preheat. Prepare a 9-inch greased springform pan and wrap a double thickness of heavy duty foil, about 18 inches square, around the pan. Mix sugar and cookie crumbs together;

add in butter. Press mixture onto the bottom of the prepared pan.
- For the cheesecake filling, put chocolate chips in the microwave and set it on high for about 1 minute until melted. Beat sugar and cream cheese together until smooth. Add flour and blend all well. Add the eggs and vanilla and beat on low speed just until combined. Measure 2 cups batter and mix in coffee liqueur; add in melted chocolate chips and mix until combined. Pour this on the prepared crust. In the remaining batter, add Irish cream liqueur. Spoon over chocolate layer. Take a larger baking pan and add 1 inch of hot water. Place the springform pan inside.
- Bake in the oven for 60 to 75 minutes, until the surface of the cheesecake appears dull while the center is just set. Remove pan from water bath and transfer to a wire rack to cool for 10 minutes. Remove the foil and using a knife, loosen the sides from the pan. Cool for another 1 hour then refrigerate overnight. Cover the pan when it's been completely cooled.
- Prepare a ganache to top and garnish the cheesecake. Combine the whipping cream and chocolate chips and microwave on high until chips are melted. Let the ganache cool slightly then remove rim from the pan. Spread ganache on chilled cheesecake.

Nutrition Information

- Calories: 485 calories
- Total Carbohydrate: 44 g
- Cholesterol: 118 mg

- Total Fat: 31 g
- Fiber: 1 g
- Protein: 6 g
- Sodium: 280 mg

Neapolitan Cheesecake

""Swirled or layered dark and white chocolate, and strawberry cheesecake on a crumb base. Serve it alone or put strawberry preserve on top or ganache.""
Serving: 12 | Prep: 40m | Ready in: 5h45m

Ingredients

- Crumb Crust:
- 1 cup chocolate cookie crumbs
- 3 tbsps. butter, melted
- Vanilla-White Chocolate Filling:
- 2 oz. white chocolate, chopped
- 1 (8 oz.) package cream cheese, softened
- 1/4 cup white sugar
- 1 egg
- 1/2 tsp. vanilla extract
- Bittersweet Chocolate Filling:
- 1 (8 oz.) package cream cheese, softened
- 1/4 cup white sugar
- 1 egg
- 1/4 tsp. vanilla
- 2 oz. bittersweet chocolate, chopped
- Strawberry Filling:
- 1 (8 oz.) package cream cheese
- 1/4 cup white sugar
- 1 egg
- 1/2 tsp. strawberry extract
- 1/3 cup strawberries, mashed

Direction

• Prepare the oven by preheating to 350°F (175°C). Combine in a small bowl the melted butter and chocolate cookie crumbs. Push down into the bottom of 9 inch springform pan. Place in the preheated oven and bake for 8 minutes; place on a wire rack to cool.

• To make vanilla-white chocolate filling: put white chocolate in a metal bowl over barely boiling water or in a glass bowl in the microwave to melt, whisking frequently; reserve. Whip 1/4 cup sugar and 8 oz. of cream cheese in a medium bowl until turns smooth. Put in 1/2 tsp. of vanilla and 1 egg until combined. Add white chocolate mixture into the batter and mix then reserve.

• To make the dark chocolate filling: place chocolate in a metal bowl over barely boiling water or in a glass bowl in the microwave to melt, whisking frequently; reserve. Whip 1/4 cup sugar and 8 oz. cream cheese in a separate bowl until smooth. Add in 1/4 tsp. vanilla and 1 egg and mix well until blended. Mix in melted chocolate.

• To make strawberry filling: combine in a third bowl the 1/4 cup sugar and 8 oz. cream cheese until become smooth. Mix in 1/2 tsp. strawberry extract and 1 egg; mix in mashed strawberries.

• Prepare the oven by preheating to 400°F (200°C).

• Place the white-chocolate vanilla cheesecake batter into the prepared crust. Then put dark chocolate and strawberry batters to layer (see Cook's note). Put in the preheated oven and bake for 10 minutes, then lower the temperature to 300°F (150°C), and keep on baking for 50 minutes, or until center is almost set when shaken.

• Take pan from the oven, instantly run a paring knife around the edge to loose, and allow to cool fully. Place in the refrigerator until chilled before taking from the pan.

Nutrition Information

• Calories: 378 calories;
• Total Carbohydrate: 27.2 g
• Cholesterol: 117 mg
• Total Fat: 27.7 g
• Protein: 7 g
• Sodium: 263 mg

New York-style Cheesecake

""A well-loved recipe of mine for New York-style cheesecake and consists a special technique for allowing the citrus-kissed cake done in the oven, so that no crack appears when the cake cools.""
Serving: 12 | Prep: 15m | Ready in: 4h15m

Ingredients

- 3 tbsps. melted butter
- 18 graham crackers, crushed
- 1/4 cup all-purpose flour
- 1 cup sour cream
- 1 tbsp. vanilla extract
- 4 (8 oz.) packages cream cheese
- 1 1/2 cups white sugar
- 2/3 cup milk
- 4 eggs
- 1 tsp. finely grated lemon zest
- 1 tsp. finely grated orange zest

Direction

- Prepare the oven by preheating to 350°F (175°C).
- Prepare a 9-inch springform pan and lightly grease the sides and bottom.
- Combine in a bowl the melted butter and graham cracker crumbs until equally moistened. Then press the crumb mixture into the bottom and about 1/2-inch up the sides of the springform pan.

- Beat vanilla extract, sour cream and flour in a bowl. Reserve.
- In a large bowl, mix sugar and cream cheese using a wooden spoon until equally combined for 3 to 5 minutes.
- Pour milk into cream cheese mixture and beat until just mixed.
- Mix in eggs, one at a time, whisking well after every addition.
- Mix in sour cream mixture, orange zest and lemon zest; beat until just combined.
- Put mixture into the prepared springform pan.
- Place in the preheated oven and bake for about 1 hour until the edges have nicely puffed and the surface of the cheesecake is firm except for a small spot in the middle that will shake once the pan is gently moved.
- Once cheesecake is finish, switch off the oven and allow to cool in the oven for 3 to 4 hours. This avoids any cracks from appearing on the top of the cheesecake.

Nutrition Information

- Calories: 556 calories;
- Total Carbohydrate: 46.9 g
- Cholesterol: 161 mg
- Total Fat: 37 g
- Protein: 10.5 g
- Sodium: 408 mg

No-bake Cheesecake

""Error to prevent when prepping no-bake cheesecake Creating no-bake cheesecake is so marvelously easy that time it seems difficult to mess it up, and while that's mostly fact, there are a couple things that will make your cake from good to perfect. Keep it from overmixing. I tries mixing my filling once in the food processor after chilling the crust, only the result is a super-soft cheesecake waiting the next day. Chill, avoid to bake the crust. If you have heard about crumb crusts you'll observe that this one has a higher proportion of butter to graham cracker crumbs. This creates for a sturdy crust when refrigerated, but would make for a soggy baked crust. Don't hurry it. Prior mixing, your cream cheese needs to be at a room temperature, and the finished filing really needs to chill overnight. Beating cold cream cheese into the filling will end up in little lumps. Properly chill the filling to set into sliceable sections, at least 4 hours but ideally overnight. Serving a No-Bake Cheesecake You want to cut and serve no-bake cheese while it is cold. This pie won't do well at a room temperature for longer than 30 minutes before it softened considerably unlike classic cheesecake. As for toppings, the sky is the limit. On my own, I love fruit preserves or fresh fruit, but a drizzle of caramel or chocolate is not bad at all. You might want a layer of slightly sweetened sour cream or Greek yogurt for a flavor more reminiscent of typical classic sour cream cheesecake. Prep Ahead: you can create this cheesecake up to 2 days in advance and refrigerated.

Storage: store the leftover cheesecake, securely wrapped, for up to 5 days in the refrigerator, but note that after 2 days the crust will soften significantly."

Ingredients

- 20 sheets Graham crackers
- 2 tbsps. packed brown sugar
- 3/4 stick unsalted butter, melted
- 450 grams cream cheese, at room temperature
- 1 can sweetened condensed milk
- 2 tbsps. freshly squeezed lemon juice
- 1 tbsp. vanilla extract

Direction

- Preparation:
- Create the crust: In a food processor fitted with the blade attachment, put the salt, sugar and graham crackers and pulse into an equal crumb, about 10 pulses. Add in the butter and blend to combine. The mixture should come together in your hand when squeezed.
- Push down the crust into the pan; place the crust mixture into a 9-inch springform pan. Push down the crumbs equally over the bottom and 1 inch up the sides of pan, using a heavy-bottomed cup as necessary to press the mixture into the pan.
- Crust chilling: place in the refrigerator for 10 minutes. In the meantime, make the filling.

• Create the filling: In a large bowl, put the cream cheese and use an electric mixer to beat on medium speed until turn smooth. Put in the vanilla, lemon juice and sweetened condensed milk and keep on beating for about 2 minutes until fully smooth.

• Chill the filling: place the filling into the crust and use an offset spatula to smooth the top. Put in the refrigerator for at least 4 hours, but ideally overnight. Take from the pan and serve: prior serving, take the sides of the springform pan. Slice the cheesecake using a long, thin knife dipped in hot water then dried.

No-bake Chocolate Cheesecake

"Milky way candy bars is so fantastic! Everybody in our family love this eye-candy dessert that is always gone in a flash."
Serving: 8-10 servings. | Prep: 50m | Ready in: 50m

Ingredients

- 1 envelope unflavored gelatin
- 1 cup cold milk
- 4 Milky Way candy bars (2.05 oz. each), sliced
- 1-1/2 cups finely crushed chocolate wafers
- 1/4 cup butter, melted
- 2 packages (8 oz. each) cream cheese, softened
- 2 tbsps. sugar
- 1 tsp. vanilla extract
- 1 cup heavy whipping cream
- Whipped topping and fresh raspberries or fresh strawberries

Direction

- Bloom the gelatin in a big sauce pan by mixing it with milk; set aside for 1 minute. Add the candy bars. Stir until they are melted, and the gelatin is dissolved for about 5 minutes. Then cool for 45 minutes or until room temperature.
- In another bowl, combine wafer crumbs and butter. Grease a 9-inch springform pan, then pour and press the wafer mixture on it to form a crust; set aside.

• Beat the sugar, cream cheese and vanilla in a separate large bowl until smooth. Then add the cream and chocolates mixture. Beat for 4 minutes on high speed. Transfer the mixture onto the prepared crust. Cover and let sit in the refrigerator for at least 8 hours or overnight.
• Slowly run a knife around the edge of the pan to loosen up the sides; unlock and remove the side of the pan. Garnish and serve with whipped topping and berries.

Nutrition Information

- Calories: 327 calories
- Total Carbohydrate: 21 g
- Cholesterol: 74 mg
- Total Fat: 25 g
- Fiber: 1 g
- Protein: 5 g
- Sodium: 247 mg

No-bake Chocolate Chip Cannoli Cheesecake

"This refreshing and tasty cheesecake is perfect for summer. It won't add heat in the house cause you don't need to use the oven."
Serving: 8 servings. | Prep: 25m | Ready in: 25m

Ingredients

- 1 package (4 oz.) cannoli shells
- 1/2 cup sugar
- 1/2 cup graham cracker crumbs
- 1/3 cup butter, melted
- FILLING:
- 2 packages (8 oz. each) cream cheese, softened
- 1 cup confectioners' sugar
- 1/2 tsp. grated orange zest
- 1/4 tsp. ground cinnamon
- 3/4 cup part-skim ricotta cheese
- 1 tsp. vanilla extract
- 1/2 tsp. rum extract
- 1/2 cup miniature semisweet chocolate chips
- Chopped pistachios, optional

Direction

- In a food processor, process cannoli shells until it forms coarse crumbs. Mix in cracker crumbs, sugar and melted butter; Process just until combined. Press down the mixture onto the bottom and sides of a greased 9-in. pie plate. Chill until firm for about 1 hour.

- Combine the first four filling ingredients, beat until combined. Mix in extracts and ricotta cheese. Add in chocolate chips. Spread into crust.
- Cover and place in the refrigerator for about 4 hours until set. Garnish with pistachios if desired.

Nutrition Information

- Calories: 548 calories
- Total Carbohydrate: 51 g
- Cholesterol: 88 mg
- Total Fat: 36 g
- Fiber: 1 g
- Protein: 8 g
- Sodium: 292 mg

Orange Bliss Cheesecake

""A fine orange-flavored filling contrasts finely with a chocolate-crumb crust. Everyone remark on the marvelous taste and color all the time.""
Serving: 8 servings. | Prep: 25m | Ready in: 25m

Ingredients

- 1 cup chocolate wafer crumbs
- 3 tbsps. butter, melted
- 1/2 cup orange juice
- 1 envelope unflavored gelatin
- 3 packages (8 oz. each) cream cheese, softened
- 3/4 cup sugar
- 1 cup heavy whipping cream, whipped
- 1 tbsp. grated orange zest
- Mini chocolate chips and sliced orange wedges, optional

Direction

- Mix butter and crumbs; press onto the bottom of a 9-inch springform pan that is ungreased. Place in the oven and bake for 10 minutes at 350°F. Let cool. Mix gelatin and orange juice in a saucepan; allow to stand for 5 minutes. Stir and cook over low heat until gelatin is melted. Let cool for 10 minutes. In the meantime, whisk sugar and cream cheese in a bowl until fluffy and light; slowly add gelatin mixture. Whisk on low speed until well combined. Let chill for about 3 minutes until partly set (look carefully-mixture will set up instantly). Cautiously fold in orange zest and whipped cream. Scoop into the crust. Let chill for 6 hours or overnight. Use knife to run around edge of pan to loosen, just before serving. Take off the sides of pan. Decorate with oranges and chocolate chips if want.

Orange Chip Cheesecake

"Adapting and mixing recipes led to this creamy creation. The distinctive citrus flavor greatly complemented this chocolate treat."
Serving: 8 servings. | Prep: 15m | Ready in: 40m

Ingredients

- 12 oz. cream cheese, softened
- 1/2 cup sugar
- 2 eggs, lightly beaten
- 1/2 tsp. salt
- 1/2 tsp. orange extract
- 3/4 to 1 cup miniature semisweet chocolate chips
- 1 chocolate crumb or graham cracker crust (9 inches)
- TOPPING:
- 1-1/2 cups (12 oz.) sour cream
- 2 tbsps. sugar
- 1/2 tsp. vanilla extract
- 1 can (11 oz.) mandarin oranges, drained
- Additional chocolate chips

Direction

- Set oven at 375 degrees. Take a large bowl and cream sugar and cream cheese until smooth. Add in eggs and beat on low speed just until combined. Add orange extract and salt and stir just until blended. Fold chocolate chips into the mixture. Pour filling over the prepared crust then bake for 20 minutes or until the

center is nearly set. Remove pan from the oven then increase its temperature to 425 degrees.
- In a large bowl, combine the sugar, sour cream and vanilla. Spread mixture on top of the cheesecake then bake again for another 5 minutes. Take out pan from the oven and transfer to a wire rack. Set aside and cool for 15 minutes then refrigerate overnight. To serve, garnish with additional chocolate chips and oranges.

Nutrition Information
- Calories: 519 calories
- Total Carbohydrate: 49 g
- Cholesterol: 128 mg
- Total Fat: 33 g
- Fiber: 2 g
- Protein: 8 g
- Sodium: 417 mg

Orange Chocolate Cheesecake

""Oranges and white chocolate are best together in this recipe.""
Serving: 12-16 servings. | Prep: 30m | Ready in: 01h35m

Ingredients

- 2 cups vanilla wafer crumbs (about 60 wafers)
- 6 tbsps. butter, melted
- 1/4 cup sugar
- FILLING:
- 4 packages (8 oz. each) cream cheese, softened
- 1 cup sugar
- 1 cup (8 oz.) sour cream
- 4 eggs
- 10 oz. white baking chocolate, melted
- TOPPING:
- 1 cup (8 oz.) sour cream
- 3 tbsps. sugar
- 1/2 to 1 tsp. orange extract
- 2 cans (11 oz. each) mandarin oranges, well drained

Direction

- Mix the first three ingredients; push down onto the bottom and 1-1/2 inch up and the sides of a 10-inch springform pan that is greased. Place in the oven and bake for 10 minutes at 350°F; fully cool. Mix sour cream, sugar and cream cheese in a large bowl until smooth. Add eggs, beat on low speed just until combined. Stir in chocolate.

• Put into crust. Put the pan on a baking sheet. Place in the oven and bake for 350°F; for 1 to 1-1/4 hours or until middle is almost set. Allow to cool at a room temperature for about 2 hours. Mix extract. Sugar and sour cream; place over filling then spread. Place in the oven and bake for 5-7 minutes at 450°F or until set. Let it chill for 1 hour, uncovered. Pile oranges on cheesecake. Place in the refrigerator, covered for at least 4 hours. Keep leftovers in the refrigerator.

Nutrition Information

- Calories: 321 calories
- Total Carbohydrate: 35 g
- Cholesterol: 102 mg
- Total Fat: 18 g
- Fiber: 0 g
- Protein: 4 g
- Sodium: 165 mg

Peanut Butter Cheese Torte

""“A well-loved recipe with my family for so long. I mainly love the fact that you do not need to bake it, and who doesn't melt for the mixed of chocolate and peanut butter?”"
Serving: 14-16 servings. | Prep: 20m | Ready in: 20m

Ingredients

- CRUST:
- 1 cup graham cracker crumbs
- 1/4 cup packed brown sugar
- 1/4 cup butter, melted
- 1/2 cup finely chopped peanuts
- FILLING:
- 2 cups creamy peanut butter
- 2 packages (8 oz. each) cream cheese, softened
- 2 cups sugar
- 2 tbsps. butter, softened
- 2 tsps. vanilla extract
- 1-1/2 cups heavy whipping cream, whipped
- CHOCOLATE TOPPING:
- 4 oz. semisweet chocolate chips
- 3 tbsps. plus 2 tsps. brewed coffee
- Chopped peanuts, optional

Direction

- Mix all crust ingredients. Then press onto the bottom and halfway up the sides of a 10-inch springform pan. Let it chill.
- To make filling, whip for about 2 minutes in a large bowl the vanilla, butter, sugar, cream cheese, and peanut butter on high until smooth. Fold in whipped cream. Cautiously scoop into the crust; put in the refrigerator for 6 hours or overnight.
- To make topping, melt chocolate with coffee in a microwave until it turns smooth. Then spread over chilled torte. Keep in the refrigerator for about 30 minutes until firm. Decorate with chopped peanuts if wished.

Nutrition Information

- Calories: 545 calories
- Total Carbohydrate: 45 g
- Cholesterol: 58 mg
- Total Fat: 38 g
- Fiber: 3 g
- Protein: 11 g
- Sodium: 278 mg

Peanut Butter Cheesecake

"The combination of chocolate and peanut butter with the crunchy and creamy, sweet and salty taste keeps this cheesecake with a pretzel crust so addictive." Serving: 12-14 servings. | Prep: 20m | Ready in: 01h15m

Ingredients

- 1-1/2 cups crushed pretzels
- 1/3 cup butter, melted
- FILLING:
- 5 packages (8 oz. each) cream cheese, softened
- 1-1/2 cups sugar
- 3/4 cup creamy peanut butter
- 2 tsps. vanilla extract
- 3 large eggs, lightly beaten
- 1 cup peanut butter chips
- 1 cup (6 oz.) semisweet chocolate chips
- TOPPING:
- 1 cup sour cream
- 3 tbsps. creamy peanut butter
- 1/2 cup sugar
- 1/2 cup finely chopped unsalted peanuts

Direction

- Mix butter and pretzels in a small bowl. Pour the mixture into a greased 10-inch springform pan and compress onto the bottom of the pan and an inch up

each side. Put the pan on a baking sheet. Place the pan inside the oven at 350°F and bake for 5 minutes. Transfer to wire rack and let it cool.
- Whip sugar and cream cheese in a large bowl until the texture is smooth. Put in vanilla and peanut butter; combine evenly. Mix in eggs on low speed until just mixed. Mix chips in. Put on top of the crust. Put the pan back on the baking sheet.
- In a 350°F oven, bake until the middle part has almost set, about 50-55 minutes. Take out of the oven, leaving the oven on, and cool for 15 minutes.
- In making the topping, mix sugar, peanut butter, and sour cream in a small bowl. Pour the filling on top and distribute evenly. Scatter nuts on top and bake for another 5 minutes.
- Let sit on a wire rack for 10 minutes.. Loosen the cake by running a knife cautiously around the pan. For another 1 hour, let the cake cool down. Place in refrigerator for the night. Take off the pan's sides. Store remaining cake in refrigerator.

Nutrition Information
- Calories: 539 calories
- Total Carbohydrate: 54 g
- Cholesterol: 86 mg
- Total Fat: 32 g
- Fiber: 3 g
- Protein: 12 g
- Sodium: 366 mg

Peanut Butter Cup Cheesecake

"Try this dessert recipe for a holiday party. Surely it will taste yummy and looks yummy as well."
Serving: 14 servings. | Prep: 20m | Ready in: 01h15m

Ingredients

- 1-1/4 cups graham cracker crumbs
- 1/4 cup sugar
- 1/4 cup crushed cream-filled chocolate sandwich cookies
- 6 tbsps. butter, melted
- 3/4 cup creamy peanut butter
- FILLING:
- 3 packages (8 oz. each) cream cheese, softened
- 1 cup sugar
- 1 cup (8 oz.) sour cream
- 1-1/2 tsps. vanilla extract
- 3 large eggs, lightly beaten
- 1 cup hot fudge ice cream topping, divided
- 6 peanut butter cups, cut into small wedges

Direction

- Mix cookie crumbs, cracker crumbs, butter and sugar in a big bowl. In a greased 9-inch springform pan, press the mixture onto the bottom and 1-inch up the sides of the pan. Set on a baking sheet.
- Place inside the oven and bake for 7-9 minutes or until set at 350 degrees. Let it cool on a wire rack. Heat

peanut butter on high in a microwaveable bowl until it becomes soft for 30 seconds. Scatter over crust to within 1 inch of edges.

• Beat until smooth the sugar and cream cheese in a big bowl. Mix vanilla and sour cream. Add in eggs and beat on low speed until combined. Put 1 cup into a bowl and put aside. Pour excess filling over peanut butter layer.

• Place inside the microwave, heat 1/4 cup fudge topping on high for 30 seconds or until thin; fold into the reserved cream cheese mixture. Gently pour over the filling and use knife to cut through to swirl.

• Put back the pan to a baking sheet. Place in an oven and bake for 55-65 minutes at 350 degrees or until center is nearly set. Let it cool on a wire rack for 10 minutes. Gently use a knife to run around the pan's edge to loosen; Cool for 1 more hour.

• Heat in the microwave the leftover fudge topping for 30 seconds or until warmed, then spread over cheesecake. Embellish with peanut butter cups. Chill overnight. Refrigerate leftovers.

Pecan-caramel Cheesecake Pie

"I regularly make this easy to prepare cheesecake pie. Up until the last piece, my husband and my son-in-law battle for it."
Serving: 8 servings. | Prep: 10m | Ready in: 50m

Ingredients

- 2 packages (8 oz. each) cream cheese, softened
- 1/2 cup sugar
- 2 eggs
- 1 tsp. vanilla extract
- 20 caramels
- 2 tbsps. 2% milk
- 1 chocolate crumb crust (8 inches)
- 1/2 cup chopped pecans
- 1/2 cup milk chocolate chips
- Pecan halves, optional

Direction

- Beat the eggs, cream cheese and sugar in a big bowl until smooth. Mix in vanilla then put aside.
- Melt the caramels and milk in a small saucepan on low heat, then stir until smooth. Pour over the crust. Sprinkle with chopped pecans. Pour cream cheese mixture on top.
- Place in the oven and bake for 40-45 minutes at 350 degrees until center is almost set. Let it cool for 10 minutes. If desired, garnish it with pecan halves and

chocolate chips. Transfer on a wire rack to cool completely. Refrigerate leftovers.

Nutrition Information
- Calories: 573 calories
- Total Carbohydrate: 56 g
- Cholesterol: 120 mg
- Total Fat: 36 g
- Fiber: 2 g
- Protein: 10 g
- Sodium: 358 mg

Peppermint Cheesecake On A Stick

""Amaze visitors with an enjoyable holiday treat- dipped cheesecake wedges you can eat without a fork. My son jokes every time that he wants to end his job so he can sell them!""
Serving: 1 dozen. | Prep: 01h15m | Ready in: 02h15m

Ingredients

- 1-1/4 cups graham cracker crumbs
- 1/4 cup sugar
- 1/4 cup butter, melted
- CHEESECAKE:
- 4 packages (8 oz. each) cream cheese, softened
- 3/4 cup sugar
- 1/3 cup sour cream
- 1/4 cup eggnog or half-and-half cream
- 2 tbsps. cornstarch
- 1 tsp. vanilla extract
- 3 large eggs, lightly beaten
- 1 cup crushed peppermint candies (about 35 candies)
- ASSEMBLY:
- 12 wooden pop sticks
- 28 oz. semisweet chocolate, chopped
- 3 tbsps. shortening
- 1/2 cup green candy coating disks, melted
- 1/4 cup red candy coating disks, melted

Direction

- Prepare the oven by preheating to 325°F. Put a greased 9-inch springform pan on a double thickness of heavy-duty foil (about 18-in. squares). Wrap foil tightly around the pan. Put on a baking sheet.
- Combine in a small bowl the sugar and cracker crumbs; mix in butter. Then press onto the bottom of the prepared pan. Place in the preheated oven and bake for 10-12 minutes or until lightly browned. Let cool on a wire rack.
- Whisk sugar and cream cheese in a large bowl until smooth. Mix in vanilla, cornstarch, eggnog and sour cream. Put in eggs; whisk on low speed just until combined. Add in peppermint candies then fold. Place over crust. Put the springform pan in a large baking pan; put 1-inch of hot water to the larger pan.
- Bake in the oven for 60-65 minutes or until middle is just set and top looks dull. Take out springform pan from water bath. Place cheesecake on a wire rack and cool for 10 minutes. Use knife to loosen sides from pan; take off foil. Cool for 1 more hour.
- Keep in the refrigerator for overnight, then cover when fully cooled.
- Take off rim from pan. Slice cheesecake into 12 slices; cautiously insert a wooden stick into the wide end of each. Put on a waxed paper-lined 15x10x1-in. baking pan; then freeze until firm.
- Melt shortening and chocolate in a microwave; whisk until smooth. Scoop chocolate mixture over each slice until all sides are coated; let excess to drip off. (Store remaining slices in freezer until ready to dip.) Put on a

waxed paper-lined baking pan. Secure any gaps by drizzling with melted chocolate, then reheat chocolate if needed. Place in the refrigerator for 10 minutes or until set.

• Garnish with melted candy coating if wished. Keep in the refrigerator until serving time.

Nutrition Information

- Calories: 951 calories
- Total Carbohydrate: 61 g
- Cholesterol: 138 mg
- Total Fat: 64 g
- Fiber: 2 g
- Protein: 12 g
- Sodium: 356 mg

Peppermint Chip Cheesecake

""I enjoy preparing cheesecakes and regularly give them as gifts or donate them to fundraisers. This one is very desired.""

Serving: 12 servings. | Prep: 20m | Ready in: 01h10m

Ingredients

- 1 package (10 oz.) chocolate-covered mint cookies, crushed
- 3 tbsps. butter, melted
- FILLING:
- 3 packages (8 oz. each) cream cheese, softened
- 3/4 cup sugar
- 5 tsps. cornstarch
- 3 large eggs, lightly beaten
- 1 large egg yolk, lightly beaten
- 1/2 cup heavy whipping cream
- 2 tsps. peppermint extract
- 1-1/4 tsps. vanilla extract
- 3 to 4 drops green food coloring, optional
- 1 cup miniature semisweet chocolate chips
- 1/2 cup chocolate-covered mint cookies, optional

Direction

- Mix in a small bowl the butter and cookie crumbs. Then push down onto the bottom and 1-inch up the sides of a greased 9-inch springform pan.

- Whip cornstarch, sugar and cream cheese in a large bowl until turn smooth. Put in egg yolk and eggs; whisk on low speed just until mixed. Mix in the extracts, cream and if wished, food coloring. Mix in chocolate chips. Place into crust. Put the pan on a baking sheet.
- Put in the oven and bake for 50-60 minutes at 325°F or until middle is just set. Cool for 10 minutes on a wire rack. Gently run a knife around edge of pan to loosen; cool for 1 more hour. Keep for overnight in the refrigerator. Put additional crushed cookies on top if wished. Store leftovers in the refrigerator.

Nutrition Information

- Calories: 391 calories
- Total Carbohydrate: 39 g
- Cholesterol: 113 mg
- Total Fat: 25 g
- Fiber: 2 g
- Protein: 5 g
- Sodium: 166 mg

Peppermint Patty Cheesecake

"This refreshing dessert have lower fat and cholesterol, so you can indulge as much as you want."
Serving: 16 servings. | Prep: 25m | Ready in: 60m

Ingredients

- 1 cup chocolate graham cracker crumbs (about 5 whole crackers)
- 2 tbsps. reduced-fat butter, melted
- 2 packages (8 oz. each) fat-free cream cheese
- 1 package (8 oz.) reduced-fat cream cheese
- 1 can (14 oz.) sweetened condensed milk
- 3/4 tsp. peppermint extract
- 2 eggs, lightly beaten
- 12 chocolate-covered peppermint patties, divided
- 1 tsp. all-purpose flour

Direction

- Preheat oven to 325 degrees then coat a 9-inch springform pan with cooking spray. Combine butter and cracker crumbs in a small bowl. Press mixture onto the prepared pan and place it on top of a baking sheet. Bake for 8 to 10 minutes or until set. Set aside and let it cool on a wire rack.
- Meanwhile, beat the cream cheeses in a large bowl until smooth; pour in milk and extract and continue stirring. Add the eggs and beat on low speed just until blended. Take eight peppermint patties and chop it

coarsely. Toss the coarsely chopped peppermint with flour then stir into the batter. Pour batter over the crust.

- Bake for 32-40 minutes or until center is almost set at 325 degrees. Remove from the oven and let it cool on a wire rack for 10 minutes. Loosen the edge by carefully running a knife around it, then cool for another 1 hour. Once cooled, place in the refrigerator and keep it chilled overnight.
- Use the remaining peppermint patties as garnish. Cut it into quarters and arrange on top of the cheesecake. Remove the sides of the pan, cut and serve.

Nutrition Information

- Calories: 228 calories
- Total Carbohydrate: 30 g
- Cholesterol: 50 mg
- Total Fat: 8 g
- Fiber: 0 g
- Protein: 9 g
- Sodium: 296 mg

Part 2

Pistachio Cheesecake

""This attractive dessert, with its beautiful chocolate drizzle, almond crust and pistachio filling, is creamy smooth. I prepared it one Christmas Eve and everyone loves it. I have never seen cheesecake gone so fast!"" Serving: 12 -14 servings. | Prep: 15m | Ready in: 01h20m

Ingredients

- 2 cups all-purpose flour
- 1/2 cup ground almonds
- 1/2 cup cold butter
- 6 packages (8 oz. each) cream cheese, softened
- 1 can (14 oz.) sweetened condensed milk
- 2 packages (3.4 oz. each) instant pistachio pudding mix
- 5 eggs, lightly beaten
- Chocolate syrup
- Whipped cream and chopped pistachios, optional

Direction

- Mix in a small bowl the almond and flour; add in butter until crumbly. Then press onto the bottom and 1-1/4 inch up the sides of a 10-inch springform pan that is greased. Place in the oven and bake for 10 minutes at 400°F. In the meantime, beat pudding mixed, milk and cream cheese in a large bowl until smooth. Put in eggs; whisk on low speed just until mixed. Place over crust. Put the pan on a baking sheet. Lower heat to 350°F. Then bake for 55-60 minutes or until middle is just set. Put on a wire rack to cool for 10 minutes. Gently run a knife around edge of pan to loosen; cool for 1 more hour. Put in the refrigerator overnight. Cut cheesecake; drizzle slices with chocolate syrup. Decorate with pistachios and whipped cream if you want.

Nutrition Information
- Calories: 344 calories
- Total Carbohydrate: 37 g
- Cholesterol: 121 mg
- Total Fat: 18 g
- Fiber: 1 g
- Protein: 8 g
- Sodium: 269 mg

Pressure Cooker Very Vanilla Cheesecake

""Vanilla and cinnamon give this cheesecake so much taste and cooking it in the pressure cooker makes a smooth, silky texture that's hard to refuse.""
Serving: 6 servings. | Prep: 20m | Ready in: 01h25m

Ingredients

- 1 cup water
- 3/4 cup graham cracker crumbs
- 1 tbsp. plus 2/3 cup sugar, divided
- 1/4 tsp. ground cinnamon
- 2-1/2 tbsps. butter, melted
- 2 packages (8 oz. each) cream cheese, softened
- 2 to 3 tsps. vanilla extract
- 2 large eggs, lightly beaten
- TOPPING (optional):
- 4 oz. white baking chocolate, chopped
- 3 tbsps. heavy whipping cream
- Sliced fresh strawberries or raspberries, optional

Direction

- Prepare a 6-inch springform pan that was greased; put water into a 6-qt. electric pressure cooker. Combine cinnamon, 1 tbsp. sugar and cracker crumbs; mix in butter. Then press onto the bottom and about 1-inch up the sides of prepared pan.

- Beat remaining sugar and cream cheese in a separate bowl until smooth. Mix in vanilla. Put eggs; whisk on low speed just until blended. Put over crust.
- Tightly cover cheesecake with foil. Put the springform pan on a trivet with handles; lower into cooker, lock the lid; ensure that the vent is closed. Choose manual setting; modify pressure to low and set time for 1 hour and 5 minutes. Once done cooking, instantly release the pressure. The cheesecake should be shaky but set in middle.
- Take out springform pan from pressure cooker; take off foil. Let cheesecake cool on a wire rack for 1 hour. Use a knife to loosen sides from the pan. Keep in the refrigerator for overnight, then cover once fully cooled.
- To make topping, melt cream and chocolate in a microwave; stir until smooth. Slightly cool. Take out rim from springform pan. Place chocolate mixture over cheesecake. Sprinkle with berries if wished, then serve.

Nutrition Information
- Calories: 484 calories
- Total Carbohydrate: 39 g
- Cholesterol: 151 mg
- Total Fat: 34 g
- Fiber: 0 g
- Protein: 8 g
- Sodium: 357 mg

Pumpkin Cheesecake With Sour Cream Topping

""This sweet and customary pumpkin cheesecake has a sour cream on top.""
Serving: 14 | Prep: 10m | Ready in: 10h5m

Ingredients

- 1 1/2 cups graham cracker crumbs
- 1/4 cup white sugar
- 1/3 cup butter, melted
- 3 (8 oz.) packages cream cheese, softened
- 1 cup packed brown sugar
- 1 (15 oz.) can solid pack pumpkin
- 2 tbsps. cornstarch
- 1 1/4 tsps. ground cinnamon
- 1/2 tsp. ground nutmeg
- 1 (5 oz.) can evaporated milk
- 2 eggs
- 2 cups sour cream
- 1/3 cup white sugar
- 1 tsp. vanilla extract
- 1 pinch ground cinnamon, or to taste

Direction

- Prepare the oven by preheating to 350°F (175°C). Prepare a 9-inch springform pan that is lightly greased,
- Mix in a bowl the 1/4 cup white sugar and graham cracker crumbs; mix in butter. Press crust onto the

bottom and 1 1/2-inches up the sides of prepared springform pan.
- Put in the preheated oven and bake for 5 to 7 minutes until set and lightly browned. Let cool for 10 minutes.
- In the meantime, mix brown sugar and cream cheese in large bowl until smooth. Mix nutmeg, 1 1/4 tsps. cinnamon, cornstarch and pumpkin into cream cheese mixture. Gently mix in eggs and evaporated milk until just combined; put into crust. Put the pan on a baking sheet.
- Put in the preheated oven and bake for 55-60 minutes until middle is just set. In a small bowl, mix vanilla extract, 1/3 cup white sugar and sour cream. Put sour cream topping over cheesecake and spread then bake for 5 more minutes. Put on a wire rack to cool for 10 minutes, then gently run a knife around edge of pan to loosen; then cool for 1 hour and keep in the refrigerator overnight.
- Take off sides of pan; allow to stand for 30 minutes at a room temperature prior to slicing. Dust with cinnamon.

Nutrition Information
- Calories: 447 calories;
- Total Carbohydrate: 38.2 g
- Cholesterol: 108 mg
- Total Fat: 30.5 g
- Protein: 7.3 g
- Sodium: 344 mg

Quick Chocolate Chip Cheesecake

"Microwave cheesecake recipe that's so good, this serving might be good for just one person only. Great for snacks but also delicious enough to bring to your potlucks."
Serving: 8 servings. | Prep: 20m | Ready in: 20m

Ingredients

- 3/4 cup all-purpose flour
- 3/4 cup graham cracker crumbs
- 6 tbsps. sugar
- 3 tbsps. baking cocoa
- 1/2 cup butter, melted
- FILLING:
- 1 package (8 oz.) cream cheese, softened
- 2 tbsps. sugar
- 2 tbsps. 2% milk
- 1 large egg, beaten
- 1/2 cup plus 2 tbsps. miniature semisweet chocolate chips, divided

Direction

- Prepare a large bowl and combine all your dry ingredients together - the cracker crumbs, flour, sugar, and cocoa; add butter and mix it in. Measure 3/4 cup of the mixture to be used for the topping later, set it aside. Grease a 9-in. microwave-safe pie plate and press onto it the remaining mixture. Without covering the pie plate, microwave on high temperature setting for 1-2 minutes or until the crust has set.

• For the cheesecake filling, combine cream cheese, sugar and milk together and beat until smooth. Add an egg and beat on low speed just until combined. Once egg has been incorporated, add 1/2 cup of chocolate chips. Spread cheese mixture evenly over the prepared pie crust. Sprinkle remaining chocolate chips and the crumb mixture that was reserved earlier.

• Still uncovered, microwave the cheesecake on high temperature for 3-4 minutes or an inserted thermometer in the center reads 160 degrees, the cheesecake is ready. Cool for 1 hour on a wire rack then refrigerate until chilled. For best result, take cheesecake out of the refrigerator and kept at room temperature for 10 minutes before cutting.

Nutrition Information

- Calories: 405 calories
- Total Carbohydrate: 38 g
- Cholesterol: 88 mg
- Total Fat: 27 g
- Fiber: 2 g
- Protein: 6 g
- Sodium: 225 mg

Raspberry & White Chocolate Cheesecake

"My mother bakes this cheesecake a lot since it's so great and lovely. She considers this cheesecake as her "go-to" recipe. She wanted me to try making it in the future."

Serving: 16 servings. | Prep: 40m | Ready in: 02h25m

Ingredients

- 1 package (10 oz.) frozen sweetened raspberries, thawed
- 1 tbsp. cornstarch
- CRUST:
- 1 cup all-purpose flour
- 2 tbsps. sugar
- 1/2 cup cold butter
- FILLING:
- 4 packages (8 oz. each) cream cheese, softened
- 1-1/2 cups sugar
- 1-1/4 cups heavy whipping cream
- 2 tsps. vanilla extract
- 2 large eggs, lightly beaten
- 12 oz. white baking chocolate, melted and cooled

Direction

- Blend the cornstarch and raspberries in a small saucepan. Boil the mixture, stirring constantly for 1-2 minutes until the mixture is thick. Use a fine-mesh

strainer to drain the mixture in a bowl. Discard the seeds. Let the mixture cool completely.
• Set the oven and preheat at 350 degrees F. Lay a double thickness of heavy-duty foil (18-inches square) in a working surface and wrap the foil around the greased 9-inches springform pan.
• Combine sugar and flour in a small bowl. Cut butter into the mixture until crumbly. Press the mixture onto the greased pan. To bake the crust, place the pan with the mixture on a baking sheet and bake for 20-25 minutes until the crust is golden brown. Transfer on a wire rack to cool. Adjust the oven temperature to 325°F.
• Beat sugar and cream cheese in a big bowl until smooth. Stir in vanilla and cream. Beat in eggs and whisk at low speed until the egg is incorporated. Mix in cooled chocolate. Spread half of the mixture all over the crust. Spread also half of the raspberry puree on its top. Drizzle on its top the remaining mixture of the batter and drop tablespoonfuls of the remaining puree over it. Use a knife to swirl the batter.
• Once the mixture is set in a springform pan, place the pan on a big baking pan and pour hot water into the bigger pan, about an inch of water. Let it bake inside the oven for 1 3/4-2 hours until its edges are golden and fixed. Make sure that the middle of the cheesecake should jiggle once moved. Transfer the springform pan on a wire rack and let it cool for 10 minutes. Use a knife to loosen the edges of the cheesecake. Remove the foil and set aside for 1 hour to cool. Store it inside the

fridge overnight. Before serving, remove the rim from the pan.

Nutrition Information
- Calories: 570 calories
- Total Carbohydrate: 45 g
- Cholesterol: 134 mg
- Total Fat: 41 g
- Fiber: 1 g
- Protein: 8 g
- Sodium: 247 mg

Raspberry Chocolate Cheesecake

"This special treat is perfect for any occasion since it has a taste of some dark chocolate and elegantly displays its red raspberries."

Serving: 12 servings. | Prep: 40m | Ready in: 40m

Ingredients

- 2 cups chocolate wafer crumbs (about 38 wafers)
- 1/3 cup sugar
- 1/2 cup butter, melted
- FILLING:
- 1 envelope unflavored gelatin
- 3/4 cup cold water
- 2 cups heavy whipping cream
- 3 packages (two 8 oz., one 3 oz.) cream cheese, softened
- 1/3 cup sugar
- 4 oz. semisweet chocolate, melted and cooled
- 1 cup fresh or frozen raspberries
- Fresh raspberries and mint, optional

Direction

- Mix together the sugar, butter and wafer crumbs. In a 9-inch greased springform pan, press mixture up sides 1 inch and on the bottom Let it rest on the side.
- Place the gelatin over the cold water in a small pot. Let it rest for about a minute. On low heat, cook and stir it until it's completely melted. Let it cool slightly.

- Whisk some cream in a big bowl until it forms stiff peaks. Set it aside. In a different big bowl, mix the sugar and cream cheese; mix in the cooled gelatin. Divide this mixture in half and spread the other half mixture in a separate bowl.
- To one bowl, add by folding melted chocolate and 1/2 of the whipped cream; dump it onto the prepared crust. While in the other bowl, add by gently folding the raspberries together with the remaining whipped cream; dump it onto the chocolate layer. Store it in the refrigerator for about 6 hours or overnight.
- Loosen from the pan by slowly running the knife around the edges. Take off sides of the pan and decorate it with mint and berries, if you desire.

Nutrition Information

- Calories: 472 calories
- Total Carbohydrate: 33 g
- Cholesterol: 97 mg
- Total Fat: 36 g
- Fiber: 2 g
- Protein: 6 g
- Sodium: 306 mg

Raspberry Ribbon Cheesecake

"A yummy treat of creamy cheesecake, chocolate crust, raspberry center and topping. A good-looking cake with a wonderful taste!"
Serving: 12-16 servings. | Prep: 30m | Ready in: 01h05m

Ingredients

- 2 cups chocolate wafer crumbs
- 1/3 cup butter, melted
- 3 tbsps. sugar
- RASPBERRY SAUCE:
- 2-1/2 cups fresh or frozen unsweetened raspberries, thawed
- 2/3 cup sugar
- 2 tbsps. cornstarch
- 2 tsps. lemon juice
- FILLING/TOPPING:
- 3 packages (8 oz. each) cream cheese, softened
- 1/2 cup sugar
- 2 tbsps. all-purpose flour
- 1 tsp. vanilla extract
- 2 large egg whites
- 1 cup heavy whipping cream
- 2 to 3 tbsps. orange juice
- 1-1/2 cups fresh or frozen unsweetened raspberries, thawed

Direction

- Mix the first three ingredients. In a greased 9-inch springform pan, press the mixture on bottom and refrigerate for an hour or until firm.
- Using a blender, make a puree with raspberries. Use a sieve to remove seeds; discard the seeds. To make 1 cup, add water if needed.
- Mix sugar and cornstarch in a saucepan. Add the raspberry juice and bring to boiling. Stir for 2 minutes until thick. Remove from the heat. Add lemon juice and stir. Set aside.
- Mix cream cheese, flour, sugar, and vanilla until smooth in a big bowl. Beat in egg whites on low speed until just combined. Mix in cream.
- Put half of the mixture in the crust. Finish with 3/4 cup raspberry sauce (cover remaining sauce and refrigerate). Slowly put remaining filling over sauce.
- Bake for 35-40 minutes at 375 degrees or until middle is almost set. Take out from oven and loosen crust from pan with a knife. Let cool for an hour on wire rack.
- Chill overnight. Put orange juice in the refrigerated raspberry sauce and slowly fold in raspberries. Dollop over cheesecake.

Nutrition Information

- Calories: 286 calories
- Total Carbohydrate: 33 g
- Cholesterol: 46 mg

- Total Fat: 16 g
- Fiber: 3 g
- Protein: 3 g
- Sodium: 174 mg

Red Velvet Cheesecake

""Make an amazing combo of red velvet cake and cheesecake. Enjoy parties and occasions with this cake that can be easily divided or make a two in one flavored cake!""

Serving: 16 | Prep: 15m | Ready in: 2h15m

Ingredients

- Cake Layer:
- 2 1/2 cups all-purpose flour, sifted
- 1 tsp. salt
- 1 tsp. baking soda
- 1 tbsp. unsweetened cocoa powder
- 1/2 cup vegetable oil
- 2 eggs
- 1 tsp. vanilla extract
- 1 tsp. white vinegar
- 1 1/2 cups white sugar
- 1 cup buttermilk
- 2 tbsps. red food coloring
- 2 tbsps. water
- Cheesecake Layer:
- 4 (8 oz.) packages cream cheese, softened
- 1 2/3 cups white sugar
- 1/4 cup cornstarch
- 2 eggs
- 1 tbsp. vanilla extract
- 3/4 cup heavy whipping cream

Direction

• Preheat oven to 175°C (350°F). Grease two 9-inch springform pans with cooking spray.
• In a big bowl, sift together salt, flour, baking soda, and cocoa powder. Whisk two eggs, vinegar, oil, vanilla extract, white sugar and buttermilk in, mix thoroughly. Add water and food coloring, whisk. Transfer half of batter in each pan.
• Bake cake for about 30 minutes or until inserted toothpick comes out clean.
• Set cake aside and let cool. Beat cream cheese in a bowl with an electric mixer until smooth. Add cornstarch and sugar, beat again until creamy. One by one, add 2 remaining eggs beating after every addition. Mix in vanilla; whisk heavy cream in by hand until blended thoroughly. Divide batter and transfer over each cake layer in each pan.
• Bake for 30 to 45 minutes until slightly brown. Let it cool for an hour on a wire rack. Cover and chill for another hour.

Nutrition Information

• Calories: 555 calories;
• Total Carbohydrate: 59.3 g
• Cholesterol: 124 mg
• Total Fat: 32.1 g
• Protein: 8.6 g
• Sodium: 428 mg

Rhubarb Swirl Cheesecake

"This is my favorite dessert, as well as my husbands'! The combination of our two favorites; cheesecake and chocolates; together with the rhubarb that balance out the sweetness is so divine." Serving: 12-14 servings. | Prep: 40m | Ready in: 01h40m

Ingredients

- 2-1/2 cups thinly sliced fresh or frozen rhubarb
- 1/3 cup plus 1/2 cup sugar, divided
- 2 tbsps. orange juice
- 1-1/4 cups graham cracker crumbs
- 1/4 cup butter, melted
- 3 packages (8 oz. each) cream cheese, softened
- 2 cups sour cream
- 8 oz. white baking chocolate, melted
- 1 tbsp. cornstarch
- 2 tsps. vanilla extract
- 1/2 tsp. salt
- 3 large eggs, lightly beaten

Direction

- Combine orange juice, 1/3 cup of sugar and rhubarb in a saucepan; bring to a boil. Reduce to low heat and simmer while stirring until the rhubarb is tender and the sauce is thickened. Set aside.

- Meanwhile, in a small bowl, combine together cracker crumbs and butter; mix well. Press onto the bottom of a greased 9-inch springform pan to create a crust. Place on a baking sheet and bake at 350°F for 7-9 minutes or until the crust is lightly browned. Take out of the oven and cool on a wire rack.
- In a large bowl, cream and beat together the cream cheese and the remaining sugar until smooth. Add in sour cream, white chocolate, cornstarch, vanilla and salt; mix well until fully incorporated. Add eggs; don't over beat, mix just until the eggs are incorporated. Pour half of the filling into the crust. Top with half of the prepared rhubarb sauce; gently swirl in the rhubarb sauce using the tip of the knife to make swirls. Top with the remaining filling and rhubarb sauce and repeat the swirl pattern.
- Place the pan on a heavy duty foil (18 in. square) wrap the foil around the pan. Place the pan on a larger pan and slowly add 1 in. of hot water. Bake at 350°F for 60-70 minutes or until the center is almost set.
- Cool on a wire rack for 10 minutes then carefully run the knife on the edge of the pan to release the sides; cool for an additional 1 hour. Cover and refrigerate overnight. Keep leftovers in the refrigerator.

Nutrition Information

- Calories: 264 calories
- Total Carbohydrate: 22 g
- Cholesterol: 94 mg
- Total Fat: 17 g

- Fiber: 1 g
- Protein: 5 g
- Sodium: 244 mg

Rich Chocolate Cheesecake

"This treat will satisfy the chocolate cravings of even hordes of kids and grandkids. Easily serve up to 16 people."

Serving: 16 servings. | Prep: 20m | Ready in: 60m

Ingredients

- 1-1/2 cups chocolate wafer crumbs (about 24 wafers)
- 1/4 cup butter, melted
- 2 tbsps. sugar
- 1/4 cup finely chopped almonds
- FILLING:
- 3 packages (8 oz. each) cream cheese, softened
- 3/4 cup sugar
- 3 large eggs
- 1/3 cup strong brewed coffee
- 1 tsp. vanilla extract
- 3/4 cup baking cocoa
- 1 cup (6 oz.) semisweet chocolate chips
- TOPPING:
- 1 cup (8 oz.) sour cream
- 2 tbsps. brown sugar
- 1 tsp. vanilla extract
- 1/2 cup sliced almonds

Direction

- Preheat oven at 375 degrees. Combine the first four ingredients in a bowl. In a 9-inch springform pan, press crust mixture onto the bottom of the pan and 1-inch up the sides. Set the pan aside. In a large bowl, combine sugar and cream cheese and beat until smooth. Stir in eggs then beat on low speed just until combined. Stir in vanilla and coffee. Next, add cocoa and beat just until blended. Stir then add the chocolate chips.

• Take the prepared pie crust and pour the mixture into it. Place pan on a baking sheet then bake for 30 to 35 minutes at 375 degrees, or until the center is nearly set.

• Remove the pan from the oven then raise its temperature to 425 degrees. Blend together the brown sugar, sour cream, and vanilla until smooth. Spread over the cheesecake while it's still warm and garnish by sprinkling nuts on top. Put it back to the oven and bake for another 10 minutes or until it has lightly browned.

• Let the cheesecake cool on a wire rack for 10 minutes. Then, loosen the sides by carefully running a knife around the edge of the pan. Cool for another 1 hour then refrigerate overnight. Take off sides of the pan and refrigerate the leftovers.

Nutrition Information

- Calories: 304 calories
- Total Carbohydrate: 31 g
- Cholesterol: 73 mg
- Total Fat: 19 g
- Fiber: 2 g
- Protein: 6 g
- Sodium: 153 mg

Rich Chocolate Mousse Cheesecake

""This type also present an irresistible chocolate mousse, as if cheesecake wasn't enough of a satisfaction. It's lovely, do-ahead dessert for any occasions.""

Serving: 12 servings. | Prep: 02h00m | Ready in: 02h30m

Ingredients

- 1-1/4 cups graham cracker crumbs
- 3 tbsps. sugar
- 3 tbsps. baking cocoa
- 1/3 cup butter, melted
- CHEESECAKE LAYER:
- 12 oz. cream cheese, softened
- 3/4 cup sugar
- 2 large eggs, lightly beaten
- 1 cup (8 oz.) sour cream
- 3 tsps. vanilla extract
- 3 tsps. coffee liqueur
- MOUSSE AND TOPPING LAYERS:
- 1 envelope unflavored gelatin
- 1/4 cup cold water
- 4 large egg yolks
- 3/4 cup 2% milk
- 1/3 cup sugar
- 1-1/2 tsps. instant coffee granules
- 4 oz. semisweet chocolate, chopped
- 1 tbsp. light rum

- 1-1/2 tsps. vanilla extract, divided
- 2 cups heavy whipping cream
- 1/4 cup confectioners' sugar
- GARNISH:
- 5 oz. dark chocolate candy coating, chopped
- 5 oz. white candy coating, chopped

Direction

- Mix in a small bowl the butter, cocoa, sugar and cracker crumbs; press onto the bottom of a 9-inch springform pan that is greased. Place in the oven and bake for 10 minutes at 350°F. Place on a wire rack to cool. To make cheesecake: mix sugar and cream cheese in a large bowl until smooth. Put in eggs; whisk on low speed just until mixed. Mix in the coffee liqueur, vanilla and sour cream; whisk just until mixed. Place over crust. Put the pan on baking sheet. Place in the oven and bake for 30-35 minutes or until middle is just set. Place on a wire rack to cool for 10 minutes. Gently run a knife around edge of pan to loosen; cool for 1 more hour. Fully cool in the refrigerator. To make mousse and topping: drizzle gelatin over water in a small bowl: allow to stand for 1 minute or until softened. Mix in a small saucepan the coffee granules, sugar, milk and egg yolks. Stir and cook over medium heat until mixture achieved 160°F, or is thick enough to cover the back of a metal spoon. Separate from the heat; mix in gelatin until melted. Mix in the 1/2 tsp. vanilla and chocolate until chocolate is melted.

- Place into a small bowl. Then set the bowl in larger bowl of ice water, stir occasionally until thickened. Meanwhile, in a large bowl, whisk cream until starts to thicken. Put in the remaining vanilla and confectioner's sugar; whisk until form a stiff peaks. Fold half of cream into mousse mixture; place over cheesecake and spread. Put remaining cream on top. Place in the refrigerator, covered, for overnight. To make chocolate curl garnish: melt dark chocolate candy coating in a microwave; whisk until smooth. Spread a thin layer over baking sheet and scrape a fork through chocolate. Allow to stand at room temperature until set. Repeat with white candy coating; gently spread over dark candy coating. Allow to stand at room temperature just until set. Holding a sturdy metal spatula or dough scraper at 45° angle, scrape over the top of the chocolate to make stripe curls. Garnish cake with curls.

Nutrition Information

- Calories: 677 calories
- Total Carbohydrate: 57 g
- Cholesterol: 218 mg
- Total Fat: 47 g
- Fiber: 1 g
- Protein: 8 g
- Sodium: 230 mg

S'more Cheesecake

"The most requested dessert during snacks, birthdays and any gathering has a very simple and unique recipe. Try to make this tasty and delicious dessert and your kids will surely love it."
Serving: 12 servings. | Prep: 20m | Ready in: 01h05m

Ingredients

- 2-1/4 cups graham cracker crumbs (about 36 squares)
- 1/3 cup sugar
- 1/2 cup butter, melted
- FILLING:
- 2 packages (8 oz. each) cream cheese, softened
- 1 can (14 oz.) sweetened condensed milk
- 2 tsps. vanilla extract
- 3 large eggs, lightly beaten
- 1 cup (6 oz.) miniature semisweet chocolate chips
- 1 cup miniature marshmallows
- TOPPING:
- 1 cup miniature marshmallows
- 1/2 cup semisweet chocolate chips
- 1 tbsp. shortening

Direction

- Mix sugar and cracker crumbs in a little bowl; mix butter in. Place it in a 10-inch springform pan and press

mixture up the sides 1 3/4 inches and on bottom. Set it aside.
• Whisk in milk, vanilla and cream cheese on a large bowl until smoothen. On low speed, beat in eggs until completely mixed. Add in marshmallows and chocolate chips; dump into crust. Spread it onto the baking pan.
• Let it bake at 325°F for at least 40 to 45 minutes until the center is nearly set. Sprinkle on marshmallows and bake it another 4 to 6 minutes until the marshmallows get puffy.
• In the meantime, dissolve shortening and chocolate chips in a microwave or heavy saucepan. Stir until it smoothens. Sprinkle it on top of the marshmallows.
• Let the pan cool on a wire rack for about 10 mins. Loosen from pan by running a knife carefully around the edges. Cool for another hour. Place it in the refrigerator overnight. Remove the sides of the pan and serve. Be sure to refrigerate any leftovers.

Nutrition Information
- Calories: 486 calories
- Total Carbohydrate: 57 g
- Cholesterol: 106 mg
- Total Fat: 27 g
- Fiber: 2 g
- Protein: 8 g
- Sodium: 292 mg

Salted Caramel Cappuccino Cheesecake

""I've become a coffee junkie after spending years of living in Seattle! I had to move across the country for a time, so made this cheesecake with the tastes of espresso, coffee and salted caramel. It raised me up on days when I felt blue about leaving one of the world's perfect coffee places.""
Serving: 12 servings. | Prep: 30m | Ready in: 01h25m

Ingredients

- 1 package (9 oz.) chocolate wafers
- 1 cup (6 oz.) semisweet chocolate chips
- 1/2 cup packed brown sugar
- 2 tbsps. instant espresso powder
- 1/8 tsp. ground nutmeg
- 1/2 cup butter, melted
- FILLING:
- 3 packages (8 oz. each) cream cheese, softened
- 1 cup packed brown sugar
- 1/2 cup sour cream
- 1/4 cup Kahlua (coffee liqueur)
- 2 tbsps. all-purpose flour
- 2 tbsps. instant espresso powder
- 4 large eggs, lightly beaten
- TOPPING:
- 1/2 cup hot caramel ice cream topping
- 1/2 tsp. coarse sea salt

Direction

- Prepare the oven by preheating to 350°F. On a double thickness of heavy-duty foil (about 18-inch square), put a greased 9-inch springform pan. Tightly wrap foil around the pan.
- In a food processor, put the first five ingredients; cover and process until it forms fine crumbs. Gently add melted butter, pulsing until mixed. Then place the mixture onto the bottom and 2-inch up the sides of prepare pan and press.
- Beat brown sugar and cream cheese in a large bowl until it becomes smooth. Mix in espresso powder, flour, Kahlua and sour cream. Put in eggs; whisk on low speed just until combined. Place into crust. Put springform pan in a large baking pan; put 1 in. hot water to the larger pan.
- Put in the preheated oven and bake for 55-65 minutes or until the middle is just set and top looks dull. Take out springform pan from water bath; take off the foil. Put cheesecake on a wire rack to cool for 10 minutes; use a knife to loosen sides from the pan. Cool for 1 more hour. Put in the refrigerator for overnight, covering once fully cooled.
- Drizzle caramel topping over cheesecake. Place in the refrigerator for at least 15 minutes. Take off the rim from the pan. Sprinkle with sea salt just before serving.

Nutrition Information

- Calories: 618 calories

- Total Carbohydrate: 64 g
- Cholesterol: 160 mg
- Total Fat: 38 g
- Fiber: 2 g
- Protein: 9 g
- Sodium: 530 mg

Special Pleasure Chocolate Cheesecake

""I love making cheesecakes when I have time. As a matter of fact, I've turn up with a few of my own recipes, and one of them won second prize at a local bake-off competition. I enjoy this fail-proof dessert since it's so simple to make and has just the right combination of ingredients to create a "special pleasure" for appetite!""
Serving: 24 servings. | Prep: 20m | Ready in: 60m

Ingredients

- 1 package (18 oz.) ready-to-bake refrigerated triple-chocolate cookie dough
- 1 package (8 oz.) milk chocolate toffee bits
- 1 package (9-1/2 oz.) Dove dark chocolate candies
- 3 packages (8 oz. each) cream cheese, softened
- 1 can (14 oz.) sweetened condensed milk
- 3/4 cup (6 oz.) vanilla yogurt
- 4 eggs, lightly beaten
- 1 tsp. vanilla extract
- Whipped cream

Direction

- Allow dough to stand for 5-10 minutes at room temperature to soften. Then press nine pieces of dough into an ungreased 13x9-inch baking dish (keep remaining dough for another use). Reserve 2 tbsps.

toffee bits for garnish; sprinkle remaining toffee bits over dough.

• Melt chocolate candies in a microwave; stir until smooth. Mix yogurt, milk and cream cheese in a large bowl until it turns smooth. Put in eggs; whisk on low speed just until mixed. Stir in melted chocolate and vanilla. Place over crust.

• Place in the oven and bake for 40-45 minutes at 350 degrees F or until middle is nearly set. Put on a wire rack to cool. Keep in the refrigerator for 4 hours or overnight. Decorate with whipped cream and reserved toffee bits.

Nutrition Information

- Calories: 290 calories
- Total Carbohydrate: 32 g
- Cholesterol: 65 mg
- Total Fat: 16 g
- Fiber: 1 g
- Protein: 5 g
- Sodium: 149 mg

Spiderweb Cheesecake

"Style your cake with this web effect form just by pulling a toothpick through the rings of the melted chocolate. This sweet treat is a must serve for any special occasions and gathering and will never fail your guests."

Serving: 6-8 servings. | Prep: 30m | Ready in: 30m

Ingredients

- 1 envelope unflavored gelatin
- 1/4 cup cold water
- 2 packages (8 oz. each) cream cheese, softened
- 1/2 cup sugar
- 1/2 cup heavy whipping cream
- 1 tsp. vanilla extract
- 1 chocolate crumb crust (8 or 9 inches)
- 2 tbsps. semisweet chocolate chips
- 1 tbsp. butter

Direction

- Add gelatin over water in a small saucepan and let it rest for about 60 seconds. Heat the gelatin and mix until its completely melted. Take off heat and let it cool a little. Mix in a bowl sugar and cream cheese until turns smooth. Slowly add vanilla, cream and the gelatin mixture, and blend it until smooth. Gently pour it over the crust.

- Dissolve the butter and chocolate chips in a microwave; stir it until smooth. Place it into a heavy-duty zip lock bag and cut a tiny hole in its corner. On the center of the cheesecake, draw a circle of chocolate and pipe evenly a 1/2-in. apart thin concentric circles over the filling. Starting from the center, slowly pull a toothpick through the circles toward the outer edge and then clean the toothpick. Repeat the steps to make a web pattern. Seal it with a cover before placing it in the refrigerator for 2 or more hours before slicing it.

Spiderweb Pumpkin Cheesecake

""A Halloween treat for all indeed.""
Serving: 12 | Prep: 20m | Ready in: 1h40m

Ingredients

- 1 1/4 cups chocolate wafer crumbs
- 1/4 cup butter, melted
- 3 (8 oz.) packages cream cheese, softened
- 3/4 cup white sugar
- 3 eggs
- 1 1/2 cups canned pumpkin pie filling
- 1 tbsp. cornstarch
- 1 cup sour cream
- 2 (1 oz.) squares semisweet chocolate
- 2 tsps. vegetable oil

Direction

- Prepare the oven by preheating to 350°F (175°C).
- In a bowl, combine melted butter and chocolate wafer crumbs; push down onto the bottom of a 9-inch springform pan.
- Beat sugar and cream cheese in a large bowl using an electric mixer until it turns smooth. Mix in eggs, one at a time, until just combined. Mix in cornstarch and pumpkin pie filling; place over chocolate wafer crust.
- Put in the preheated oven and bake for 50-55 minutes until center is just set. Place sour cream over the top of warm cheesecake then spread; allow to cool.

• Put oil and chocolate in a microwave-safe bowl and melt in a microwave for 1 minute; mix until fully melted. Then drizzle chocolate onto sour cream topping in a spiral design, beginning from the middle; draw a toothpick outward, from middle to edges, through circles to make a web. Take off the side of the pan and serve.

Nutrition Information

- Calories: 455 calories;
- Total Carbohydrate: 35.5 g
- Cholesterol: 127 mg
- Total Fat: 32.6 g
- Protein: 7.9 g
- Sodium: 359 mg

Strawberries & Cream Pie

"This strawberry pie is a hit whenever I brought it to family events like dinner or to church activities. I also bring with me a copy of the recipe because everyone asks for it."

Serving: 8 servings. | Prep: 20m | Ready in: 20m

Ingredients

- 1 cup (6 oz.) semisweet chocolate chips, divided
- 3 tsps. shortening, divided
- 1 graham cracker crust (10 inches)
- 1 package (8 oz.) cream cheese, softened
- 1/2 cup sugar
- 1/2 cup sour cream
- 1 tsp. vanilla extract
- 1 carton (8 oz.) frozen whipped topping, thawed
- 2 cups fresh strawberries, halved
- 1/2 cup seedless strawberry jam

Direction

- Melt 3/4 cup chocolate chips and 2 tsps. shortening in a microwave; mix until smooth. Brush over the crust. Put in the refrigerator to firm up.
- Beat sugar, cream cheese, vanilla and sour cream in a small bowl until smooth. Fold in the whipped topping. Scoop into crust. Chill for 1 hour.
- Garnish strawberries over pie. Melt jam in a microwave; brush over the top. Melt and stir leftover

chocolate chips and shortening until smooth. Drizzle over pie. Chill in the refrigerator.

Nutrition Information

- Calories: 539 calories
- Total Carbohydrate: 63 g
- Cholesterol: 41 mg
- Total Fat: 30 g
- Fiber: 2 g
- Protein: 5 g
- Sodium: 213 mg

Swirled Raspberry & Chocolate Cheesecake

"Use a foaming power of eggs to have a fluffier and lighter cheesecake. Whisk egg whites until it forms stiff peaks, and then fold it into the cream cheese mixture. Adding eggs bring more volume into the mixture. It's my family's favorite."
Serving: 12 servings. | Prep: 40m | Ready in: 01h35m

Ingredients

- 4 eggs
- 1-1/2 cups graham cracker crumbs
- 1/4 cup confectioners' sugar
- 1/3 cup butter, melted
- FILLING:
- 1 cup fresh raspberries
- 1/2 tsp. sugar
- 3 packages (8 oz. each) cream cheese, softened
- 1 can (14 oz.) sweetened condensed milk
- 1 tsp. vanilla extract
- 1 cup (6 oz.) semisweet chocolate chips, melted and cooled
- Additional fresh raspberries, optional

Direction

- Separate the eggs and let it stand in room temperature for about half an hour. Place the greased 9-inches springform pan over an 18-inch double thick

and heavy-duty square shaped foil. Fold the foil tightly around the pan.
• Mix confectioners' sugar and cracker crumbs in a small bowl. Blend in butter. Press the mixture onto the prepared pan. Process the sugar and raspberries in a blender until smooth. Strain the mixture and discard the seeds.
• Set the oven to 325°F for preheating. Whisk the cream cheese in a big bowl until smooth. Stir in vanilla and milk. Add the egg yolks and whisk at low speed until well-incorporated. Get 1 tbsp. of the mixture and add it into the raspberry puree. Get 1/2 of remaining mixture and transfer into another bowl. Blend in cooled chocolate.
• Whisk egg whites in a big bowl until it forms stiff peaks. Use a spatula to spread half of the egg whites into the chocolate mixture until white streaks are no longer visible. Pour the mixture over the crust.
• Add the remaining half of the egg whites in the plain cheese mixture. Pour the mixture over the chocolate layer. Spread tablespoonfuls of raspberry mixture on its top and use a knife to swirl the filling.
• Place the pan in a big baking pan after all the preparations. Add boiling water into the larger pan, about 1-inch.
• Let it bake inside the preheated oven for 55-65 minutes until the top looks dull and the center is all fixed. Remove the pan from the water bath and discard the foil. Transfer the pan into the wire rack and let it cool for 10 minutes. Use a knife to loosen the edges of

the cheesecake. Set aside to cool for 60 more minutes before placing it inside the fridge. Refrigerate it overnight.

- Remove the cheesecake from the pan and serve it with more raspberries.

Nutrition Information

- Calories: 505 calories
- Total Carbohydrate: 42 g
- Cholesterol: 157 mg
- Total Fat: 35 g
- Fiber: 3 g
- Protein: 11 g
- Sodium: 334 mg

Taffy Apple Cheesecake Pie

""I made this dessert a lot of times during apple season. But it's literally perfect for any occasion. The pie mixes the excellent tastes of cheesecake and caramel apples.""
Serving: 8-10 servings. | Prep: 55m | Ready in: 01h30m

Ingredients

- 3/4 cup packed brown sugar, divided
- 2 tbsps. butter
- 5 cups thinly sliced peeled tart apples
- 21 caramels
- 1/2 cup half-and-half cream
- 1 package (8 oz.) cream cheese, softened
- 1-1/2 tsps. vanilla extract
- 1 tsp. pumpkin pie spice, divided
- 1 egg, lightly beaten
- 1 unbaked deep-dish pastry shell (9 inches)
- 3/4 cup chopped pecans
- 1/2 cup milk chocolate chips, chopped
- 2 cups whipped topping

Direction

- Mix in large skillet the butter and 1/4 cup brown sugar. Then cook over medium-high heat until sugar is melted, whisking occasionally. Put in apples. Cook for 12-15 minutes, uncovered or until apples are soft, whisking occasionally; strain and reserve.

- Mix in a large heavy sauce pan the cream and caramels; cook over low heat, whisking constantly. Separate from heat; keep warm. Beat in a large bowl the 1/2 tsp. pie spice, vanilla, remaining brown sugar and cream cheese until smooth. Put in egg; whisk on low speed just until mixed. Mix half of the caramel mixture into apples. Place into pastry shell. Mix chocolate chips and pecans; reserve 2 tbsps. for topping. Dust remaining pecan mixture over apples. Mix in remaining caramel mixture into cream cheese mixture. And spread over pecan mixture.
- Use foil to cover edges loosely. Place in the oven and bake for 20 minutes at 375°F. Take off the foil; continue to bake for 15-20 more minutes or until filling is set. Place on a wire rack and let cool. Then let chill for 30 minutes.
- Mix remaining pumpkin pie spice and whipped topping; spread over pie just prior serving. Dust with reserved pecan mixture. Keep leftovers in the refrigerator.

Nutrition Information
- Calories: 501 calories
- Total Carbohydrate: 57 g
- Cholesterol: 61 mg
- Total Fat: 29 g
- Fiber: 3 g
- Protein: 6 g
- Sodium: 222 mg

Tiny Cherry Cheesecakes

"These mini cheesecakes are ideal for many occasions like Christmas or weddings. I also get frequent compliments and requests for this recipe. I pack extra when I give it to my husband for lunch because he shares it with his workmates and they love it too."
Serving: 2 dozen. | Prep: 25m | Ready in: 40m

Ingredients

- 1 cup all-purpose flour
- 1/3 cup sugar
- 1/4 cup baking cocoa
- 1/2 cup cold butter
- 2 tbsps. cold water
- FILLING:
- 6 oz. cream cheese, softened
- 1/4 cup sugar
- 2 tbsps. milk
- 1 tsp. vanilla extract
- 1 large egg, lightly beaten
- 1 can (21 oz.) cherry or strawberry pie filling

Direction

- Mix sugar, cocoa and flour in a small bowl and cut in butter until the mixture becomes crumbly. Slowly add water, tossing with a fork until the dough forms a ball. Form 24 balls. Put in greased miniature muffin cups

and press down the dough onto the bottom and up the sides of each cup.
- Beat the sugar and cream cheese in a big bowl until smooth. Add vanilla and milk. Add in egg and beat on low just until combined. Scoop around 1 tablespoonful into each cup.
- Place in an oven and bake for 15 to 18 minutes at 325 degrees or until set. Transfer on a wire rack and cool for 30 minutes. Gently remove from pans to fully cool. Put pie filling on top. Keep in the refrigerator.

Nutrition Information
- Calories: 119 calories
- Total Carbohydrate: 16 g
- Cholesterol: 23 mg
- Total Fat: 5 g
- Fiber: 0 g
- Protein: 1 g
- Sodium: 57 mg

Toffee Crunch Cheesecake

"An excellent dessert for any occasion. Thick, creamy cheesecake that has chocolate coated toffee bits in the crust and topping."
Serving: 12-14 servings. | Prep: 40m | Ready in: 01h30m

Ingredients

- 1-1/2 cups graham cracker crumbs
- 2 tbsps. brown sugar
- 1/3 cup butter, melted
- 1/2 tsp. vanilla extract
- 1 cup milk chocolate English toffee bits
- FILLING:
- 3 packages (8 oz. each) cream cheese, softened
- 1 cup sugar
- 1 cup (8 oz.) sour cream
- 3 tsps. vanilla extract
- 4 eggs, lightly beaten
- TOPPING:
- 1-1/2 cups sour cream
- 1/4 cup sugar
- 1 tsp. vanilla extract
- 1/2 cup milk chocolate English toffee bits

Direction

- Mix cracker crumbs, butter, brown sugar, and vanilla in a bowl. In a greased 9-inch springform pan, press

mixture on bottom and up sides 2 inches. Bake for 6-8 minutes or until set, at 350 degrees. Let cool on wire rack. Sprinkle toffee bits on the crust.
• Mix sugar and cream cheese in a bowl until smooth. Add in vanilla and sour cream. Add eggs and beat on low speed to just blend. Put the mixture in crust. Put the pan on a baking tray.
• Bake for 50-60 minutes or until center is slightly set at 350 degrees. Let cool for 10 minutes on wire rack. Loosen edges carefully with a knife.
• For topping, mix sugar, vanilla and sour cream. Pour evenly over the cheesecake. Bake for another 5 minutes. Let cool for one-hour on wire rack. Chill overnight. Take off the sides of the pan. Top with toffee bits.

Nutrition Information
• Calories: 552 calories
• Total Carbohydrate: 42 g
• Cholesterol: 171 mg
• Total Fat: 38 g
• Fiber: 0 g
• Protein: 8 g
• Sodium: 367 mg

Topped Cheesecake Squares

"These toppings are so easy to make. You only need to microwave these a few minutes and composed of only 3 to 4 ingredients. Let your family and friends select the toppings for their cheesecake from chocolate-dipped strawberry, caramel and almonds, and fresh jam and fruit."

Serving: 9 servings. | Prep: 30m | Ready in: 60m

Ingredients

- 1-1/4 cups chocolate wafer crumbs
- 1/4 cup butter, melted
- 2 packages (8 oz. each) cream cheese, softened
- 2/3 cup plus 2 tbsps. sugar, divided
- 2 eggs, lightly beaten
- 1-1/2 tsps. vanilla extract, divided
- 1/4 tsp. almond extract
- 1 cup (8 oz.) sour cream
- CHOCOLATE STRAWBERRIES:
- 2 oz. dark chocolate candy bar
- 3 fresh strawberries
- 1 oz. white baking chocolate
- CARAMEL TOPPING:
- 6 caramels
- 1 tbsp. heavy whipping cream
- Whipped cream
- 1 tbsp. sliced almonds, toasted
- BERRY TOPPING:
- 1/4 cup seedless raspberry jam

- 6 fresh raspberries
- 6 fresh blackberries
- 6 fresh blueberries

Direction

- Mix butter and crumbs in a small bowl. Put mixture in a square 8-inch baking dish, compress tightly onto the base of the baking dish.
- Whip 2/3 cup sugar and cream cheese in a small bowl until smooth. Put in eggs. On low speed, beat until mixed evenly. Add almond extract and 1/2 tsp. vanilla; stir.
- Put on the crust. Put inside the oven and bake for 45-55 minutes at 325°F or until it has set. Let it cool down about 5 minutes.
- In the meantime, mix the rest of the vanilla and sugar with sour cream in a small bowl. Scatter evenly on the filling; bake for another 5 minutes. Transfer to a wire rack and let it cool for 1 hour. Then put inside the refrigerator for 5 hours or for a night.
- Dissolve candy bar in a microwave. Mix until the consistency is smooth. Duck in the chocolate the strawberries; drip off the excess. Line the baking sheet with waxed paper and place the dipped strawberries on it. Let them rest until set. Dissolve and stir white chocolate until the texture is smooth. Lightly sprinkle it on to your strawberries. Put in refrigerator before serving.

- When serving, slice the cheesecake into 9 squares. On three squares of the cheesecake, add the chocolate strawberries on top.
- To make the caramel topping, mix cream and caramels in a small microwave-safe bowl. Place inside the microwave for 45 seconds with no cover on high setting. Mixing it just one time. Using a spoon, scoop on 3 cheesecake squares. Put whipped cream on top; add almonds by sprinkling.
- In making berry topping, mix berries and jam in a small microwave-safe bowl. Put inside the microwave uncovered for 45 seconds on high, stirring only one time. Using a spoon, scoop on the rest of the squares.

Triple-layer Chocolate Cheesecake

""A marvelous cheesecake! This one has a yummy white chocolate flavor and chocolate crust! So pretty, visitors will be amazed.""
Serving: 12 servings. | Prep: 40m | Ready in: 01h35m

Ingredients

- 1 package (9 oz.) chocolate wafer cookies, crushed
- 3/4 cup sugar, divided
- 1/2 cup butter, melted
- 2 packages (8 oz. each) cream cheese, softened, divided
- 3 large eggs
- 1 tsp. vanilla extract, divided
- 1/3 cup packed dark brown sugar
- 2 oz. semisweet chocolate, melted and cooled
- 1-1/3 cups sour cream, divided
- 1 tbsp. all-purpose flour
- 1/4 cup chopped pecans
- 3 oz. cream cheese, softened
- 1/4 tsp. almond extract
- GLAZE:
- 5 oz. semisweet chocolate, divided
- 1/4 cup heavy whipping cream
- 1/2 cup white baking chips
- 2 tsps. canola oil
- Raspberries, optional
- Mint leaves, optional

Direction

• Mix butter, 1/4 cup sugar and wafer crumbs. Push down onto the bottom and 2-inch up the sides of 9-inch springform pan; reserve. Beat 1/3 tsp. vanilla, 1/4 cup sugar and 8-oz.package cream cheese in a small bowl. Lightly whisk 1 egg; put into cream cheese mixture and whisk on low speed just until mixed. Mix in 1/3 cup sour cream and melted chocolate. Scoop over crust. Whip 1/3 tsps. vanilla, flour, brown sugar, and second 8-oz package of cream cheese in another bowl until smooth.

• Lightly beat 1 egg; add to cream cheese mixture and beat on low speed just until combined. Mix in pecans. Gently scoop over chocolate layer. Put pan on a baking sheet. Whisk almond extract. 3-oz package of cream cheese and remaining vanilla, sour cream and sugar until smooth. Lightly whisk remaining egg; put into cream cheese mixture and whisk on low speed just until mixed. Gently scoop over pecan layer. Place in the oven and bake for 55-60 minutes at 325°F or until center is almost set. Place on a wire rack and cool for 10 minutes. Cautiously run a knife around edge of pan to loosen; let cool for 1 more hour. Place in the refrigerator overnight. To make glaze, cut up 3-oz semisweet chocolate and put in a small bowl. Place cream in a small saucepan and make it just boil. Place over chocolate; mix until turn smooth. Take off sides of springform pan; spread glaze over top of cheesecake to within 1/2-inch of edges. Place in the refrigerator until serving time. To make chocolate curls, melt left of semisweet chocolate; then use a spatula to spread into a very thin layer on a baking sheet. Let chill for 2 minutes or until set.

- Put oil and white chips in a microwave at 70% power for 1 minute; stir. If necessary, microwave at additional 10-15 second intervals, stirring until melted.
- Use spatula to spread into a very thin layer on second baking sheet. Let chill for 2 minutes or until set. To make curls, use a metal spatula and push firmly along the baking sheet, under the chocolate, so the chocolate curls as it is pushed. (if allow to stand for a few minutes at a room temperature if chocolate is too firm to curl; then refrigerate again if it turns too soft.) Gently put each chocolate curl using a toothpick on a waxed paper-lined baking sheet. Place in the refrigerator until ready to use. Pile chocolate curls on top of cheesecake just before serving. Decorate with mint and raspberries if want.

Nutrition Information
- Calories: 624 calories
- Total Carbohydrate: 51 g
- Cholesterol: 148 mg
- Total Fat: 44 g
- Fiber: 2 g
- Protein: 9 g
- Sodium: 347 mg

Turtle Cheesecake

""People refused to think that these ultra-creamy cheesecake was low in fat, but we checked the numbers three times, and they're delightfully correct. The calories are still a bit high, but fat-free cream cheese and light butter drop the fat count to only 20 percent of the recipe's calories (less than half of a regular slice), and goodies like chocolate chips and caramel sauce increased the flavor.""

Ingredients

- 2 tbsp roughly chopped pecans
- Butter-flavored vegetable-oil cooking spray
- 20 chocolate graham crackers, finely ground
- 4 tsp light butter, melted
- 2 packages (8 oz. each) fat-free cream cheese
- 1 package (8 oz.) lowfat cream cheese
- 2 whole eggs
- 6 egg whites
- 21 oz. fat-free sweetened condensed milk (about 1 1/2 cans)
- 1/2 cup unsweetened cocoa powder
- 3/4 cup semisweet chocolate chips
- 1 cup caramel topping

Direction

- Prepare the oven by preheating to 325°F. Place pecans on a cookie sheet and toast for 10-12 minutes; take from the oven. Increase oven heat to 375°F. Use a cooking spray to coat a 9-inch springform pan. Use your hands to mix butter and cookies in a bowl, then press into pan. Bake in the preheated oven for 10 minutes; take from the oven. Puree egg whites, eggs and cream cheese in a food processor. Put in cocoa and milk and blend until smooth and all one color. Mix in chocolate chips and process by turning the machine on and off a few times. Place into and pan and bake for 40 minutes until just set. Take from the oven. Let cool for 30 minutes in the fridge. Take from pan and put pecans and caramel on top.
- Nutritional review per serving: 0.7g fiber, 13.9g protein, 57.7g carbohydrates, 8.1g fat (4.1g saturated fat, 358 calories.
- Nutritional review given by self.

Turtle Pumpkin Cheesecake

"A combination of cheesecake and pumpkin pie makes this Thanksgiving dessert is so delectable."
Serving: 16 servings. | Prep: 30m | Ready in: 01h25m

Ingredients

- 1-1/2 cups crushed gingersnap cookies (about 30 cookies)
- 1/4 cup butter, melted
- Filling:
- 4 packages (8 oz. each) cream cheese, softened
- 1 cup packed brown sugar
- 2/3 cup sugar
- 1 can (15 oz.) solid-pack pumpkin
- 2 tbsps. all-purpose flour
- 2 tsps. pumpkin pie spice
- 4 large eggs, lightly beaten
- Topping:
- 4 oz. bittersweet chocolate, chopped
- 2 tbsps. butter
- 1/2 cup chopped pecans, toasted
- 1/2 cup caramel sundae syrup
- Whipped cream, optional

Direction

- Mix butter and cookie crumbs in a small bowl. Grease a 10-inch springform pan and pour the mixture compressing it onto the pan's base and 1 inch up each side. On a baking sheet, put the pan. Place inside a 325°F oven and bake for 8-10 minutes. Transfer to a wire rack to cool down.

• Whip the sugar and cream cheese in a large bowl, until the consistency is smooth. Mix flour, spice, and pumpkin. Put in the eggs. On a low speed setting, whip the mixture until just mixed. Transfer mixture in crust. Put the pan back on the baking sheet.

• Place inside the oven to bake mixture until the middle part has almost set, about 55-65 minutes. Transfer to a wire rack to cool down, about 10 minutes. Loosen the cake by running a knife cautiously around the pan's edges. Chill for another 1 hour. Put in refrigerator for a night. Take off the pan's sides.

• Dissolve butter and chocolate in a microwave; mix until the consistency is smooth. Add caramel syrup, chocolate mixture, with pecans on top of cheesecake, and if you want, add whipped cream.

Nutrition Information

- Calories: 492 calories
- Total Carbohydrate: 47 g
- Cholesterol: 127 mg
- Total Fat: 32 g
- Fiber: 2 g
- Protein: 8 g
- Sodium: 336 mg

Tuxedo Cheesecake

"Impress your guests with the pairing of vanilla and chocolate in an elegant layered cheesecake."
Serving: 16 | Prep: 15m | Ready in: 6h15m

Ingredients

- 1 1/4 cups chocolate cookie baking crumbs
- 1/4 cup butter, melted
- 2 (250 g) packages PHILADELPHIA Chocolate Brick Cream Cheese, softened
- 3/4 cup white sugar, divided
- 3 eggs, divided
- 1 (250 g) package PHILADELPHIA Brick Cream Cheese, softened
- 1/2 tsp. vanilla extract
- 4 oz. BAKER'S Semi-Sweet Chocolate
- 2 oz. BAKER'S White Chocolate

Direction

- Preheat oven to 350°F (175°C).
- Blend butter and baking crumbs; in 9-in. springform pan bottom press mixture.
- Mix 1/2 cup sugar and chocolate cream cheese until combined in a bowl with mixer. Add in 2 eggs on low speed, one at a time, just blend after each one. Spread over the crust. Place is freezer for 15 minutes or until texture is thick.

- Mix remaining sugar and plain cream cheese until combined in a bowl with a mixer. Beat in egg on low speed until just blended. Spread over the chocolate batter to evenly coat.
- Bake for 40-45 minutes or center is slightly set. Loosen the sides with a knife. Let cool before removing pan rim. Chill for 4 hours.
- Melt chocolate separately according to instructions on package. Line baking sheet with parchment paper and spread 1/4-in. thick the semi-sweet chocolate. Put small spoonsful of the white chocolate on top. With a knife, gently swirl the chocolate. Let cool until firm.
- Slice chocolate in different shapes. Use chocolate to garnish cheesecake before serving.

Nutrition Information

- Calories: 342 calories;
- Total Carbohydrate: 30.2 g
- Cholesterol: 90 mg
- Total Fat: 22.8 g
- Protein: 5.6 g
- Sodium: 236 mg

Two-tone Cheesecake

""Ended with this creamy cheesecake when I was searching to make an original one for a contest. And it won Grand Champion!""

Serving: 12 servings. | Prep: 25m | Ready in: 01h25m

Ingredients

- 1-1/2 cups chocolate graham cracker crumbs
- 6 tbsps. sugar
- 6 tbsps. butter, melted
- FILLING:
- 4 packages (8 oz. each) cream cheese, softened
- 1-3/4 cups sugar
- 3/4 cup heavy whipping cream
- 4 eggs, lightly beaten
- 6 oz. semisweet chocolate, melted and cooled
- TOPPING:
- 4 oz. semisweet chocolate, finely chopped
- 1/2 cup heavy whipping cream

Direction

- Mix in a large bowl the butter, sugar and cracker crumbs. Then push down onto the bottom of a greased 10-inch springform pan. Put on a baking sheet. Place in the oven and bake for 10 minutes at 325°F. Put on a wire rack and cool.

- Beat in a large bowl the sugar and cream cheese until smooth. Slowly mix in the cream. Put in eggs; whisk on low speed just until blended.
- Take 3-1/2 cups to a small bowl; cautiously mix in melted chocolate. Place filling over the crust. Cautiously pour remaining filling over chocolate layer. Place in the oven and bake for 1 to 1-1/4 hours at 325°F or until center is nearly set.
- Put on a wire rack and cool for 10 minutes. Gently run a knife around the edge of the pan to loosen; cool for 1 more hour. In the meantime, put chopped chocolate in a small bowl.
- Put the cream in a small saucepan and bring it just to a boil. Place over chocolate; stir until smooth; slightly cool; cautiously pour over cheesecake. Chill overnight, covered. Take off sides of the pan.

Nutrition Information
- Calories: 432 calories
- Total Carbohydrate: 48 g
- Cholesterol: 141 mg
- Total Fat: 26 g
- Fiber: 1 g
- Protein: 5 g
- Sodium: 208 mg

Vanilla Bean Cheesecake With Chocolate Ganache

"I made this version of cheesecake recently during the birthday of my mother. She loves it so much! There's a trace of orange in the chocolate crust that makes each chomp worth relishing."
Serving: 16 servings. | Prep: 50m | Ready in: 01h50m

Ingredients

- 2 cups chocolate graham cracker crumbs (about 16 graham crackers)
- 4 tsps. grated orange zest
- 1/3 cup butter, melted
- FILLING:
- 3 packages (8 oz. each) cream cheese, softened
- 1 cup sugar
- 1 cup sour cream
- 1 vanilla bean or 1 tsp. vanilla extract
- 3 large eggs, lightly beaten
- TOPPING:
- 1 cup semisweet chocolate chips
- 2/3 cup heavy whipping cream
- 2 cups fresh raspberries

Direction

- Turn on the oven and preheat it at 325°F. Wrap the greased 9-inches springform pan in a double thick, heavy-duty foil (about 18-inch square).

- Whisk orange zest and cracker crumbs in a small bowl. Mix in butter. Spread the mixture onto the bottom and 2-inches up the sides of the greased pan. Store it inside the refrigerator for 5 minutes.
- Mix sugar and cream cheese in a big bowl until smooth. Stir in sour cream. Cut the vanilla bean lengthwise and scrape the seeds from the middle using the tip of a knife; add it in the cream cheese mixture. Beat in eggs and whisk at low speed just until combined. Pour the mixture into the chilled crust. Place the pan in a big baking pan with an inch of hot water.
- Bake the cheesecake for 60-70 minutes until the top looks dull and the center is set. Take the pan away from the water bath and transfer it on a wire rack to cool for 10 minutes. Loosen the edges of the pan using a knife. Discard the foil and let it cool for 60 more minutes. Cover once it is cool and refrigerate it for the whole night.
- Put the chocolate chips in a small bowl for the topping. Boil the cream in a small saucepan. Spread the hot cream over the chocolate chips and whisk the mixture until smooth. Let it cool down to room temperature for 10 minutes until the mixture achieves its thick spreading consistency.
- Remove the rim from the pan. Pour the chocolate mixture on the cheesecake. Store it inside the refrigerator for 1 hour until it's all fixed. Before serving, top the cheesecake using raspberries.

Vanilla Chip Dessert

"This delectable dessert is just a piece of cake to prepare which has a creamy stuffing and vanilla chips flavor. "It is decorated at times with chocolate shavings"."

Serving: 15 servings. | Prep: 25m | Ready in: 30m

Ingredients

- 3 cups crushed vanilla wafers (about 90 wafers)
- 1/2 cup butter, melted
- 3 tbsps. brown sugar
- 1 package (10 to 12 oz.) white baking chips
- 2 packages (8 oz. each) cream cheese, softened
- 2 cups (16 oz.) sour cream
- 1 carton (8 oz.) frozen whipped topping, thawed
- Chocolate ice cream topping, optional

Direction

- Mix butter, brown sugar and wafer crumbs in a big bowl and flatten it on a greased 13x9-inch baking pan. Put it in the oven and bake for 5 to 8 minutes or until it turned light brown at 350°F. Let it cool.
- On the other hand, melt white chips in a microwave and mix until smooth. Allow it to cool.
- In a separate big bowl, beat sour cream and cream cheese together until smooth, and put in melted chips. Blend well and fold in.

• Pour the mixture over the prebaked crust, cover and chill until set or for 2 hours. Sprinkle some chocolate toppings (optional).

Very Vanilla Slow Cooker Cheesecake

"Use a slow cooker to create this vanilla and cinnamon flavored cheesecake. It's delicious taste and smooth texture will make it hard for you to resist it"
Serving: 6 servings. | Prep: 40m | Ready in: 02h40m

Ingredients

- 3/4 cup graham cracker crumbs
- 1 tbsp. sugar plus 2/3 cup sugar, divided
- 1/4 tsp. ground cinnamon
- 2-1/2 tbsps. butter, melted
- 2 packages (8 oz. each) cream cheese, softened
- 1/2 cup sour cream
- 2 to 3 tsps. vanilla extract
- 2 large eggs, lightly beaten
- TOPPING:
- 2 oz. semisweet chocolate, chopped
- 1 tsp. shortening
- Miniature peanut butter cups or toasted sliced almonds

Direction

- Prepare a 6-inches springform pan. Wrap a double thickness, 12 inches square heavy duty, foil around pan securely.
- In a 6 quart slow cooker, pour 1 inch of water. Place 2 pieces of 24-inches foil. Roll up the foil, starting from the longer side, to make a 1 inch wide strip and shape

it into a circle. Make a rack by putting it in the bottom of the slow cooker.
- Combine 1 tbsp. of sugar, cinnamon and cracker crumbs together in a small bowl. Add butter; 1 inch up the sides and in bottom of pan by pressing.
- Whisk the remaining sugar and cream cheese in a big bowl until it is smooth. Stir in vanilla and sour cream. Combine eggs and on low speed beat it until just mixed. Spread the mixture on the crust.
- Transfer to springform pan on the circled foil without touching the sides of the slow cooker. Using a double layer of white paper towels, cover the slow cooker and slowly place the lid over the towels. Let it cook on high heat for 2 hours while covered.
- Switch off the slow cooker and let the cheesecake rest for about an hour more, while the lid is still attached to the slow cooker.
- Remove the pan from the slow cooker as well as the foil around it. Let it cool on a wire rack for about 1 hour. Use a knife to loosen the sides from the pan; put in fridge overnight. Leave it covered until cooled completely.
- Melt shortening and chocolate inside the microwave to make topping. Stir it until smooth. Let it cool slightly; then remove the rim from the pan. Drizzle the chocolate mixture over the cheesecake together with almonds or miniature peanut butter cups.

Nutrition Information
- Calories: 565 calories

- Total Carbohydrate: 41 g
- Cholesterol: 180 mg
- Total Fat: 41 g
- Fiber: 1 g
- Protein: 10 g
- Sodium: 351 mg

White Chocolate Cheesecake

"This is an unbelievably rich, creamy and mild White chocolate cheesecake with the combination of cream cheese and chocolate."
Serving: Makes 16 servings. | Prep: 40m | Ready in: 7h5m

Ingredients

- 1/2 cup butter, softened
- 3/4 cup sugar, divided
- 1-1/2 tsp. vanilla, divided
- 1 cup flour
- 4 pkg. (8 oz. each) PHILADELPHIA Cream Cheese, softened
- 3 pkg. (4 oz. each) BAKER'S White Chocolate, broken into pieces, melted, cooled
- 4 egg s
- 2 cups fresh raspberries

Direction

• 1. In a small bowl, use mixer to beat 1/2 tsp vanilla, 1/4 cup sugar and butter until it turns fluffy and light. Slowly beat in flour till blended completely then press onto bottom of a 9" springform pan. Use a fork to prick it. Bake until edge has light brown color, or for 25 minutes.

• 2. In a big bowl, beat vanilla, leftover sugar, and cream cheese using a mixer until completely blended. Add in chocolate and mix thoroughly. One at a time, add eggs, beat on low speed after each addition just until blended. Spill over crust.

• 3. Bake until it's mostly set in the middle, or for 55-60 minutes. Loosen cake by running knife around rim of pan. Cool before removing rim. Chill in fridge for 4 hours. Sprinkle raspberries on top before serving.

Nutrition Information

- Calories: 450
- Total Carbohydrate: 32 g
- Cholesterol: 145 mg
- Total Fat: 33 g
- Fiber: 1 g
- Protein: 7 g
- Sodium: 290 mg
- Sugar: 25 g
- Saturated Fat: 20 g

White Chocolate Cheesecake With Cherry Topping

"For a change, you can change the crust by using chocolate chip cookies and shortbread or vanilla wafers instead of the graham crackers. For the topping, use strawberry or other fruit instead of cherry. This recipe is very simple and versatile."
Serving: 16 servings. | Prep: 35m | Ready in: 01h40m

Ingredients

- 2-1/2 cups cinnamon graham crackers crumbs (about 13 whole crackers)
- 1/4 cup packed brown sugar
- 1/2 cup butter, melted
- FILLING:
- 4 packages (8 oz. each) cream cheese, softened
- 1-1/3 cups sugar
- 1 tsp. vanilla extract
- 4 eggs, lightly beaten
- 3 oz. white baking chocolate, finely chopped
- TOPPING:
- 1-1/2 cups (12 oz.) sour cream
- 1/4 cup sugar
- 1 oz. white baking chocolate, melted and cooled slightly
- 1 can (21 oz.) cherry pie filling
- Whipped cream

Direction

• Set the oven to 325°F for preheating. Combine brown sugar and cracker crumbs in a small bowl. Spread the mixture into the bottom along with 1 1/2-inch up the sides of the greased 10-inches springform pan. Place the pan onto a big baking sheet.
• Whisk sugar and cream cheese in a big bowl until smooth. Stir in vanilla. Beat in eggs and whisk at low speed until well-combined. Add the chocolate before pouring the mixture into the crust.
• Bake it inside the preheated oven for 55-60 minutes until the center is almost fixed. Place on a wire rack to cool for 5 minutes. While waiting, combine melted chocolate, sugar, and sour cream in a small bowl. Spread the mixture on top of the cheesecake and bake for 10 more minutes.
• Transfer on a wire rack to cool for 10 minutes. Use a knife to loosen the edges of the cheesecake. Cool for 60 more minutes. Cover and store it inside the fridge overnight.
• Remove the rim from the pan and serve with whipped cream and pie filling.

White Chocolate Cheesecake With Cranberry-orange Compote

"This pastry will take the show once you serve it on your dining table. You'll love its creamy cheese texture, perfect cranberry topping, and its orange flavor." Serving: 12 servings. | Prep: 30m | Ready in: 01h25m

Ingredients

- 1-1/2 cups chocolate wafer crumbs
- 1/4 cup butter, melted
- 2 tbsps. sugar
- FILLING:
- 3 packages (8 oz. each) cream cheese, softened
- 3/4 cup sugar
- 12 oz. white baking chocolate, chopped and melted
- 1/2 cup sour cream
- 1 tbsp. vanilla extract
- 3 large eggs, lightly beaten
- 2 tsps. grated orange zest
- CRANBERRY-ORANGE COMPOTE:
- 1 package (12 oz.) fresh cranberries
- 3/4 cup packed brown sugar
- 3/4 cup orange juice
- 1 tbsp. grated orange zest
- 1/2 tsp. ground ginger
- GARNISH:
- Sweetened whipped cream, optional

Direction

• Set the oven to 325°F for preheating. Place the greased 9-inches springform pan over an 18-inch double thick and heavy-duty square shaped foil. Secure the foil tightly around the pan and place it over the baking sheet.
• Combine sugar, butter, and wafer crumbs in a small bowl. Pour the mixture into the prepared baking pan. Bake it inside the preheated oven for 10 minutes. Transfer it onto a wire rack to cool.
• Whisk sugar and cream cheese in a big bowl until smooth. Stir in sour cream, vanilla, and melted chocolate. Whisk in egg and beat on low speed until just incorporated. Add the orange zest before pouring it over the crust. Pour boiling water into a big baking pan, about 1-inch of the pan, and submerge the springform pan.
• Let it bake inside the oven for 55-65 minutes until the top looks dull and the center is fixed. Remove the pan from the water bath and transfer it onto the wire rack. Let it cool for 10 minutes. Use a knife to loosen the sides of the cake. Remove the foil and let it cool for 1 more hour.
• While waiting, combine all the compote ingredients in a big saucepan. Cook it over moderate heat for 15 minutes until the berries pop. Allow it to cool at room temperature before spreading it all over the cheesecake. Cover the pan once it's cool and store it inside the fridge overnight. Remove the cheesecake

from the pan and serve it with whipped cream, if desired.

Nutrition Information

- Calories: 622 calories
- Total Carbohydrate: 61 g
- Cholesterol: 138 mg
- Total Fat: 38 g
- Fiber: 2 g
- Protein: 9 g
- Sodium: 333 mg

White Chocolate Lime Mousse Cake

""This cake was always on top and a hit whenever I served it at a party. Creates a beautiful presentation, baking up nice and high. The gingersnap and zippy lime tastes really come through.""
Serving: 12-16 servings. | Prep: 20m | Ready in: 20m

Ingredients

- 2 cups crushed gingersnaps (about 38 cookies)
- 2 tbsps. sugar
- 1/3 cup butter, melted
- FILLING:
- 1 envelope unflavored gelatin
- 6 tbsps. lime juice
- 9 oz. white baking chocolate, chopped
- 2-1/2 cups heavy whipping cream
- 3 packages (8 oz. each) cream cheese, softened
- 1 cup sugar
- 1 tbsp. grated lime zest

Direction

- Mix in a large bowl the butter, sugar and gingersnaps; then press onto the bottom and 1-inch up the sides of a greased 9-inch springform pan. Reserve. Drizzle gelatin over lime juice in a microwave-safe dish. Allow to stand for 1 minute. Then microwave for 10-20 seconds on high; mix until gelatin is melted. Reserve, melt chocolate with 1/2 cup cream in a microwave; mix until smooth. Slightly cool; mix in melted gelatin. Beat sugar and cream cheese in a large bowl until smooth. Gently add chocolate mixture and lime zest and combine well. Beat remaining cream in a separate bowl until form a stiff peaks. Cautiously fold into cream cheese mixture. Scoop over the crust. Then chill overnight, covered. Store leftovers in the refrigerator.

Nutrition Information

- Calories: 348 calories
- Total Carbohydrate: 30 g
- Cholesterol: 77 mg
- Total Fat: 25 g
- Fiber: 0 g
- Protein: 3 g
- Sodium: 206 mg

White Chocolate Peppermint Cheesecake

"This is the most requested dessert in our house since my kids love the taste of candy bits all over the cheesecake."

Serving: 16 servings. | Prep: 30m | Ready in: 01h45m

Ingredients

- 1-1/2 cups graham cracker crumbs
- 1 tbsp. sugar
- 1/2 cup butter, melted
- FILLING:
- 3 packages (8 oz. each) cream cheese, softened
- 1 cup sugar
- 1 tbsp. brown sugar
- 1 cup (8 oz.) sour cream
- 3 tbsps. all-purpose flour
- 1 tsp. vanilla extract
- 1 tsp. peppermint extract
- 6 eggs, lightly beaten
- 1 cup white baking chips
- 1 cup crushed peppermint candies, divided

Direction

- Grease a 10-inches springform pan and place it over a double thickness of heavy-duty foil, about 18-inches square. Wrap the foil tightly around the pan.
- Mix butter, cracker crumbs, and sugar in a big bowl. Press the mixture at the bottom and 1-inch up the

sides of the greased pan. Set the oven to 325°F and bake it for 10 minutes. Transfer on a wire rack to cool.
- Whisk sugar and cream cheese in a big bowl until smooth. Stir in extracts, flour, and sour cream. Add the eggs and whisk at low speed until well-blended. Stir in a 3/4 cup of crushed candies and chips. Pour the mixture all over the crust and top it with the remaining candies.
- Pour hot water in a big baking pan, about 1-inch of the pan. Place the springform pan into the water bath.
- Bake the cake for 1 1/4 hours until the top appears dull and the center is fixed. Remove the pan from the water bath after baking and transfer it on a wire rack. Let it cool for 10 minutes. Use a knife to loosen the edge of the cake. Let it cool for 1 more hour before placing it inside the refrigerator. Refrigerate overnight. Remove the rim from the pan. Serve.

Nutrition Information

- Calories: 430 calories
- Total Carbohydrate: 35 g
- Cholesterol: 153 mg
- Total Fat: 29 g
- Fiber: 0 g
- Protein: 7 g
- Sodium: 257 mg

White Chocolate Pumpkin Cheesecake

""This creamy and rich cheesecake is everyone's looking forward to every Thanksgiving.""
Serving: 12 servings. | Prep: 35m | Ready in: 01h25m

Ingredients

- 1-1/4 cups Oreo cookie crumbs
- 2 packages (8 oz. each) cream cheese, softened
- 2/3 cup sugar
- 2 tsps. vanilla extract
- 3 large eggs, lightly beaten
- 8 oz. white baking chocolate, melted and cooled
- 1/2 cup canned pumpkin
- 1/4 tsp. each ground ginger, cinnamon and nutmeg
- White chocolate curls and/or crushed Oreo cookies, optional

Direction

- Put a 9-inch springform pan that is greased on a double thickness heavy-duty foil (about 18-inch square). Tightly wrap foil around pan. Onto the bottom of prepared pan, press cookie crumbs; reserve. Beat vanilla, sugar and cream cheese in a large bowl until smooth. Put in eggs; whisk on low speed just until mixed. Mix in melted chocolate. Mix spices and pumpkin in a small bowl; carefully fold into cream cheese mixture. Place over crust. Put springform pan in a large baking pan; put 1 in.of hot water to larger pan.

Place in the oven and bake for 50-55 minutes at 325°F or until middle is almost set. Take springform pan from water bath. Place on a wire rack and cool for 10 minutes. Carefully run a knife around edge of pan to loosen; cool 1 hour longer. Place in the refrigerator overnight. Take off sides of pan. Decorate with chocolate curls and/or crushed cookies if want.

Nutrition Information
- Calories: 369 calories
- Total Carbohydrate: 37 g
- Cholesterol: 85 mg
- Total Fat: 23 g
- Fiber: 1 g
- Protein: 6 g
- Sodium: 230 mg

White Chocolate Pumpkin Cheesecake With Almond Topping

"A cheesecake baked and chilled overnight. It is so delicious because of the pumpkin filling on top of the mouth-watering gingersnap crust, topped with crunchy almonds."

Serving: 12 servings. | Prep: 30m | Ready in: 01h25m

Ingredients

- 1-1/2 cups crushed gingersnap cookies (about 32 cookies)
- 1/4 cup butter, melted
- 3 packages (8 oz. each) cream cheese, softened
- 1 cup sugar
- 3 eggs, lightly beaten
- 1 tsp. vanilla extract
- 5 oz. white baking chocolate, melted and cooled
- 3/4 cup canned pumpkin
- 1 tsp. ground cinnamon
- 1/4 tsp. ground nutmeg
- ALMOND TOPPING:
- 1/2 cup chopped almonds
- 2 tbsps. butter, melted
- 1 tsp. sugar

Direction

- Mix butter and gingersnap crumbs in a small bowl. Pour into a greased springform pan, 9-inch in size, and compress mixture onto the base of the pan; set it aside.

• Whisk together sugar and cream cheese in a large bowl until smooth in consistency. At a low speed, whisk in vanilla and eggs until mixed evenly. Add melted white chocolate, mix well.

• Mix spices and pumpkin; lightly mix into the cream cheese mixture by folding. Put mixture on the crust in the pan and place on a baking sheet.

• Put inside the oven at 350°F and bake until middle part has set, about 55-60 minutes. Move to a wire rack and let cool for 10 minutes. While cooling, mix the ingredients for the toppings; in a low-sided baking pan, distribute the mixture evenly. Put inside the oven for 10 minutes, mixing twice, until the color turns to golden brown. Let cool.

• Loosen the cheesecake by cautiously running a knife around the edge of the springform. Chill for 1 hour and put inside the refrigerator for the night. Keep your toppings inside an airtight container inside the refrigerator.

• Take off the sides of the pan and add topping on top of cheesecake before serving.

White Chocolate Raspberry Cheesecake

"This recipe can be a good dessert to serve in any special gatherings. You can style it with white chocolate curls if you want."
Serving: 16 | Prep: 1h | Ready in: 10h

Ingredients

- 1 cup chocolate cookie crumbs
- 3 tbsps. white sugar
- 1/4 cup butter, melted
- 1 (10 oz.) package frozen raspberries
- 2 tbsps. white sugar
- 2 tsps. cornstarch
- 1/2 cup water
- 2 cups white chocolate chips
- 1/2 cup half-and-half cream
- 3 (8 oz.) packages cream cheese, softened
- 1/2 cup white sugar
- 3 eggs
- 1 tsp. vanilla extract

Direction

- Whisk melted butter, 3 tbsps. of sugar, and cookie crumbs in a medium bowl. Spread the mixture on the bottom of a 9-inch springform pan.
- Combine the cornstarch, water, raspberries, and 2 tbsps. of sugar in a saucepan and boil for 5 minutes

until the sauce is thick. Let it drain in a mesh strainer and discard the seeds.
• Set the oven to 325°F or 165°C for preheating. Melt half-and-half and white chocolate chips into a metal bowl with a pot of simmering water over it. Make sure to stir the mixture occasionally while melting until it's smooth.
• Blend a half cup of sugar and cream cheese in a big bowl until smooth. Whisk in eggs, one at a time. Add the melted white chocolate and vanilla. Pour half of the batter over the crust. Add 3 tbsps. of the raspberry sauce over the batter. Pour another layer of cheesecake batter into the pan and top it with 3 tbsps. of raspberry sauce. Use the tip of the knife to swirl the batter to make a marbled effect.
• Let it bake inside the oven for 55-60 minutes until the filling is fixed. Let it cool completely. Cover the pan with a plastic wrap and store it inside the refrigerator for 8 hours. Remove the cheesecake from the pan and serve it together with the leftover raspberry sauce.

Nutrition Information
• Calories: 412 calories;
• Total Carbohydrate: 34.4 g
• Cholesterol: 96 mg
• Total Fat: 28.3 g
• Protein: 6.8 g
• Sodium: 226 mg

White Chocolate Strawberry Torte

""A dessert that is well-liked by family at gatherings.""
Serving: 10-12 servings. | Prep: 20m | Ready in: 20m

Ingredients

- 1 cup crushed vanilla wafers (about 30 wafers)
- 1/2 cup finely chopped almonds, toasted
- 1/4 cup butter, melted
- 12 oz. white baking chocolate, melted
- 3 cups whole medium fresh strawberries
- 4 oz. cream cheese, softened
- 1/4 cup sugar
- 1/4 cup thawed orange juice concentrate
- 1 tsp. vanilla extract
- 2 cups heavy whipping cream
- 1 tbsp. baking cocoa
- Additional strawberries, halved

Direction

- Reserve 2 tbsps. of wafer crumbs. Mix the rest of the crumbs, butter and almonds. In a 9-inch ungreased springform pan, add the mixture and compress onto the base of the pan. Put on crust 5 tbsps. of melted white chocolate; using the reserved wafer crumbs sprinkle them on top. Assemble over the crumbs the strawberries with tips up.
- Whip cream cheese in a bowl until smooth in consistency. Put in vanilla, juice concentrate and sugar.

Whip in the rest of the white chocolate. Whip cream in a different bowl until soft peaks are formed. Add in cream cheese mixture, about 2 cups; stir until well combined. Stir slowly by folding the rest of the whipped cream in. Scatter on and between strawberries. Chill inside the refrigerator covered for 3 hours or for a night.
• Loosen the cake by running a knife cautiously around the pan's edges; remove pan's sides. Assemble 4 strips of waxed paper 1-1/2-inch-wide on top. Drizzle between strips cocoa. Take off the waxed paper. Put halves of strawberries between cocoa rows.

Nutrition Information
- Calories: 321 calories
- Total Carbohydrate: 19 g
- Cholesterol: 76 mg
- Total Fat: 27 g
- Fiber: 2 g
- Protein: 4 g
- Sodium: 115 mg

White Chocolate-raspberry Mousse Cheesecake

"The flavors were blended well in this heavenly cheesecake. I always serve this as a dessert on Christmas Day, New Year's celebration, and any social gatherings."

Serving: 16 servings. | Prep: 50m | Ready in: 01h40m

Ingredients

- 2 cups graham cracker crumbs
- 1/2 cup butter, melted
- 1/3 cup sugar
- FILLING:
- 2 cups white baking chips, divided
- 3 packages (8 oz. each) cream cheese, softened
- 3/4 cup sugar
- 1/3 cup sour cream
- 1 tbsp. all-purpose flour
- 1 tsp. vanilla extract
- 3 large eggs, lightly beaten
- MOUSSE:
- 1 envelope unflavored gelatin
- 3 tbsps. cold water
- 1 tbsp. lemon juice
- 1 package (12 oz.) frozen unsweetened raspberries, thawed
- 1/2 cup sugar
- 1 large egg plus 1 large egg yolk, beaten
- 1/4 cup raspberry liqueur

- 1-1/2 cups heavy whipping cream, whipped
- Fresh raspberries, white chocolate curls and mint leaves, optional

Direction

- Grease a 9-inches springform pan and place it over a double thickness of heavy-duty foil (18-inches square), wrapping the foil tightly around the pan.
- Combine cracker crumbs, sugar, and butter in a small bowl. Pour the mixture onto the bottom of the greased pan.
- Melt 1 cup of white chips in a microwave. Stir it until smooth; set aside. Whisk cream cheese and sugar in a big bowl until smooth. Mix in flour, vanilla, and sour cream. Add the melted chips. Stir in eggs and beat at low speed until just incorporated. Add the remaining chips and pour the mixture over the crust.
- Pour hot water in a big pan, about 1-inch. Place the springform pan in a water bath and bake at 325°F for 50-60 minutes until its top appears dull and its center is just set. Transfer the springform pan on a wire rack after baking. Let it cool for 10 minutes. Run a sharp knife into the edges of the pan to loosen the cake. Let it cool for 60 more minutes.
- Mix lemon juice, cold water, and gelatin in a small bowl. Set aside for 60 seconds. In a food processor, blend the raspberries until smooth. Strain the puree to separate the seeds; discard the seeds.
- Mix a half cup of the raspberry puree and sugar in a small saucepan and heat the mixture until bubbles

appear around the pan. Pour a bit of the hot mixture in the egg mixture and bring them all back into the pan. Let it cook over low heat, whisking constantly until the mixture reaches 160°F. Remove the mixture from the heat.

- Add a bit of the hot mixture into the gelatin mixture and mix until the gelatin dissolves completely. Add the leftover hot raspberry mixture and a liqueur. Whisk in the leftover raspberry puree. Place the mixture inside the refrigerator, covered, for 30 minutes. Whisk in whipped cream. Spread the mixture over the cheesecake.
- Store the cheesecake in a fridge overnight. Loosen the sides of the pan and garnish the cheesecake with white chocolate curls, mint leaves, and raspberries if you want.

Nutrition Information
- Calories: 569 calories
- Total Carbohydrate: 46 g
- Cholesterol: 164 mg
- Total Fat: 39 g
- Fiber: 1 g
- Protein: 8 g
- Sodium: 278 mg

Chocolate Covered Strawberries

This recipe is the perfect one to use when you need a special treat in a hurry.

Ingredients
360 g white baking chips
170 g chopped semisweet chocolate
85 g chopped white chocolate
454 g strawberries with stems, washed and dried very well

Directions
Put the semisweet and white chocolates into 2 separate heatproof medium bowls. Fill 2 medium saucepans with a couple inches of water and bring to a simmer over medium heat. Turn off the heat; set the bowls of chocolate over the water to melt stirring constantly.

Once the chocolates are melted and smooth, remove from the heat. Line a cookie sheet with parchment or waxed paper. Holding the strawberry by the stem, dip the fruit into the dark chocolate, lift and twist slightly, letting any excess chocolate fall back into the bowl. Set strawberries on the parchment paper. Repeat with the rest of the strawberries.

Dip a fork in the white chocolate and drizzle the white chocolate over the dipped strawberries.

Set the strawberries aside until the chocolate sets, about 30 minutes.

Creamy Chocolate Covered Strawberries

The addition of orange liquor and heavy cream makes these strawberries positively sinful.

Ingredients
170 g sweet chocolate
44 ml heavy cream
10 ml orange flavored liquor
14 g softened, unsalted butter
454 g fresh strawberries, with stems attached

Directions
Place sweet chocolate in the top of a double boiler and set over hot water while stirring to melt the chocolate.
Add the cream, liquor, and butter and heat the mixture, stirring until smooth
Dip the strawberries in chocolate. Place on a wax paper lined dish and place in refrigerator until ready to serve.

Chocolate Covered Strawberries (2)

The milk chocolate used for these chocolate covered strawberries makes them a scrumptious dessert.

Ingredients
454 g milk chocolate chips
28 g shortening
454 g fresh strawberries with leaves

Directions
Insert toothpicks into the tops of the strawberries.
In a double boiler, melt the chocolate and shortening, stirring occasionally until smooth.
Holding them by the toothpicks, dip the strawberries into the chocolate mixture.
Turn the strawberries upside down and insert the toothpick into Styrofoam for the chocolate to cool.

Chocolate Dipped Strawberries

The piped chocolate makes these strawberries both delicious and beautiful.

Ingredients
24-30 fresh strawberries
170 g white chocolate
227 g dark chocolate

Directions
Wash and dry the strawberries, making sure the berries are fully dry as water will cause chocolate to seize up.
Melt the white chocolate in a double boiler or microwave.
Dip the strawberry in the white chocolate, holding onto the stem or "shoulders" of the strawberry. Give it a quick little twist and shake with your fingers to shake off the excess and then point it at the ceiling for a second or two to ensure that the chocolate adheres to the strawberry. Place on a piece of wax paper to let dry.
Melt the dark chocolate according to the instructions on the package. Dip the strawberry into the chocolate, making sure to let the excess drip off. Place on wax paper to dry.
Place some melted dark chocolate into a piping bag with a very small tip, or in a sealable bag with the little corner snipped off and drizzle or decorate the strawberries.

Allow to dry and cool, or place them in the freezer for 5 minutes.

Chocolate Banana Mousse

This creamy treat combines chocolate and bananas in such a delicious way that you won't even miss the sugar.

Ingredients
28 g unsweetened chocolate
237 ml evaporated skim milk
36 g granulated sugar replacement
2 egg yolks
1 g salt
5 ml vanilla extract
2 bananas, sliced

Directions
In a double boiler, mix chocolate, 59 ml milk and sugar substitute. Stir continuously until chocolate melts.
Pour a small amount of chocolate mixture over egg yolks and whisk thoroughly.
Pour the tempered eggs into the double broiler with the chocolate. Add salt and stir. Continue to cook and stir until the mixture thickens. Allow to cool.
Beat very cold milk until it is stiff. Fold the chocolate into the milk, and then fold in vanilla and banana slices. Place in containers in the freezer until the mousse is firm.

Chocolate Balls

These are easy to make and popular at parties. Take a plate of them to your next gathering or keep some in the refrigerator for a daily indulgence.

Ingredients
113 g Margarine, room temp
24 g Sugar
71 ml liquid sugar substitute
124 g flour
21 g Cocoa
2.5 g Salt
40 g Chopped nuts
19 g Raisins

Directions
Cream margarine and sugar until the mixture is light and fluffy.
Add vanilla and sugar and beat for 30 seconds at medium speed.
Blend flour, cocoa and salt before adding it to creamed mixture. Mix until blended.
Fold in nuts and raisins.
Use a small spoon to shape balls. Place them on a lined cookie sheet.
Bake for 20-25 minutes at 165 degrees C. Allow to cool.

Sugar Free Chocolate Nut Clusters

These super-simple delights are ideal for satisfying the need for something salty and sweet.

Ingredients
159 g sugar-free chocolate
121 g nuts, coarsely chopped

Directions
Place aluminum foil over a baking sheet.
Melt sugar-free chocolate in the microwave, taking care to stir occasionally to avoid scorching.
Add the nuts to the chocolate and stir until all nuts are coated.
Use a spoon to drop small amounts on the aluminum foil.
Allow to set in the refrigerator for 20 minutes.

Sugar Free Chocolate Butter Creams

These taste so rich and creamy that they seem as though they were just purchased at a candy store.

Ingredients
116 g nonfat dry milk powder
33 g cocoa
30 g paraffin wax
118 ml water
14 g shortening
15 ml liquid sugar replacement (artificial sweetener)
85 g cream cheese, softened
30 ml milk
8 ml vanilla extract
192 g equivalent of sugar substitute

Directions
Blend milk powder, cocoa and was in a blender until it forms a powder.
Put powder in a double boiler and add water. Mix completely. Add shortening.
Cook over low heat and stir continuously until wax is melted.
When the sauce is creamy and thick, remove it from the heat. Add sugar replacement.
Allow to cool a little before dipping items in chocolate.
Beat cream cheese, milk and vanilla until the mixture is fluffy. Stir in sugar substitute.

Roll mixture into balls and allow to chill in the refrigerator. Coat each ball in chocolate before placing on a piece of wax paper.

Bittersweet Chocolate Sauce

When your fruit or yogurt needs a little extra help, drizzle this chocolate sauce over the top. It's the perfect way to add a bit of chocolate to any dessert.

Ingredients
177 ml skim milk
83 g Dutch process or unsweetened cocoa
28 g margarine
10 ml vanilla
192 g sugar substitute

Directions
Slowly add milk to cocoa in a small saucepan, stirring constantly. Allow it to simmer before stirring in vanilla. Allow to cool.
Stir in sugar substitute. Refrigerate the sauce until it is time to serve.

Chocolate With Chocolate Chip Pancakes

Serve these on a weekend morning, and your entire household will wake up happy.

Ingredients
592 ml almond milk or other non-dairy milk alternative
30 ml apple cider vinegar
199 g all-purpose flour
28 g pure cocoa powder
7 g baking powder
4 g baking soda
3 g salt
60 g packed dark brown sugar
2 large eggs, lightly beaten
14 g dairy-free soy margarine, melted
135 g dairy-free chocolate chips

Directions
Whisk together almond milk and cider vinegar. Allow the mixture to thicken for 5 minutes.
Sift flour, cocoa powder, baking powder, baking soda, salt and sugar in a medium bowl.
In a separate bowl, blend almond mixture, eggs and margarine until just combined. Stir in wet ingredients, but take care not to over mix.

Scoop a small amount of batter onto a hot griddle. When bubbles form around the outside edges, flip the pancakes until they are thoroughly cooked.

Dairy Free Chocolate Pudding

This pudding is so rich and creamy that you can't tell that it's dairy free.

Ingredients
28 g cornstarch
30 ml water
355 ml soy milk
1 ml vanilla extract
48 g white sugar
29 g unsweetened cocoa powder

Directions
Make a paste by combining cornstarch and water.
Cook soy milk, vanilla, sugar, cocoa and cornstarch mixture over medium heat. Allow it to cook until it boils and thickens, stirring constantly. Remove from heat and allow it to cool for 5 minutes. Refrigerate until serving.

Lactose Free Chocolate Cake

This is the perfect chocolate cake for anyone who suffers from milk or nut allergies.

Ingredients
149 g all-purpose flour
2.5 g teaspoon salt
192 g white sugar
28 g cocoa powder
4 g baking soda
74 ml vegetable oil
15 ml white vinegar
5 ml vanilla extract
237 ml cold water
90 g semisweet chocolate chips

Directions
Mix flour, salt, sugar, cocoa powder and baking soda together in a large bowl. Add oil, vinegar and vanilla. When it is well combined, stir in cold water, and then add chocolate chips. Place the batter in a greased 20x20 centimeter pan.
Bake at 180 degrees C for 30 to 35 minutes.

Dairy Free Chocolate Chip Cookies

These are a delightful way to enjoy chocolate without worrying about the lactose content. You can also substitute applesauce for the margarine for an even healthier treat.

Ingredients
220 g dairy-free margarine
110 g brown sugar
96 g cane sugar
59 ml of soy or rice milk
10 ml vanilla
224 g flour
2.5 g salt
4 g baking soda
340 g dairy-free semisweet chocolate chips

Directions
Preheat oven to 180 degrees C. Chop chocolate and set aside.
Combine margarine with both sugars until it is smooth and fluffy. Stir in milk and vanilla.
Combine all dry ingredients in a separate bowl. Blend them into the sugar mixture. Fold in chocolate.
Drop batter on cookie sheet. Bake cookies for 9 minutes or until they are golden brown.

Dairy Free Hot Chocolate

This is a great way to enjoy lactose free chocolate on a cold, dreary day.

Ingredients
237 ml water
113 g dairy-free dark chocolate
57 g white organic sugar
710 ml plain unsweetened soymilk
2.5 ml vanilla

Directions
Whisk chocolate and water over low heat until chocolate is melted and smooth.
Stir in sugar until it has dissolved.
Increase to medium heat. Stir constantly until mixture is just about to boil. Then add soymilk and vanilla.
Cook until the drink is thick and smooth.

www.ingramcontent.com/pod-product-compliance
Lightning Source LLC
Chambersburg PA
CBHW071434070526
44578CB00001B/98